PRAISE FOR *VEG FORWARD*

"Make room for more produce in your life! I can think of few people who know their way around a vegetable like Susan: how to cook it, how to coax out all its flavor, how to transform it into something simply special, and—of course—how to make it look like a million bucks on the plate. *Veg Forward* advances plant-based cooking several steps ahead with its savvy, seasonal, (dare I say) sexy recipes, and of course the gorgeous photography you'd expect from a Spungen production. From grain dishes and soups to pizzas and desserts, not only will you *not* miss the meat—you may never need it again."

ADEENA SUSSMAN, AUTHOR OF *SABABA* AND *SHABBAT*

"The latest from America's culinary rock star, Susan Spungen is literally a cook's dream. Try the Spoonbread-Stuffed Poblanos with Tomato Cream, Cheese Blintzes with Sour Cherry Compote, Rhubarb Galettes with Hazelnut Frangipane, or the Sungold Spaghetti Carbonara. These recipes are laden with wonderful instructions, handy tips, and amazing food lore. Susan has managed to blast into the vegetable-forward movement with panache and humor—what could be better? I am totally going to make all these dishes; you will too!"

JONATHAN WAXMAN, CHEF/OWNER OF BARBUTO, NEW YORK CITY

"With this beautiful cookbook, Susan has created a blueprint for exactly the way I want to cook and eat right now, namely, with vegetables stepping into the spotlight to play the starring role. As usual, her recipes toe that magic line between stunning and simple (she shot all the photos on her iPhone, in real time!), and I've already dog-eared half the pages. This one's a keeper."

JENNY ROSENSTRACH, BESTSELLING AUTHOR OF *DINNER: A LOVE STORY* AND *THE WEEKDAY VEGETARIANS*

"A book full of vibrant, seasonal, and nourishing recipes that put vegetables front and center. I want to cook them all."

ARAN GOYOAGA, AUTHOR OF *CANNELLE ET VANILLE*

"Not only is Susan making vegetables approachable and easy in *Veg Forward*, but she's making them extremely delicious. At the end of the day, all that matters is deliciousness, and these recipes are oozing with flavor that packs a punch. Mushroom Bourguignon? Yes, please. Asparagus Pizza with Arugula Salad? You already know ya' boy is game. You see, I've had the pleasure of Susan cooking for me and of knowing how much passion she brings to her cooking and recipes; these are sure to become household staples for not just me but for many vegetable-curious and vegetarians out there in the world."

BRYAN FORD, AUTHOR OF *NEW WORLD BAKING*

"We can always trust Susan Spungen's eye for detail, color, and perfectly crisp vegetables from the farmers' market—pairing that with her exacting recipes that are genuinely doable (from Monday to Sunday!) is *Veg Forward*'s big win. From a creamy nettle sauce on pasta to smoky corn salad and peach galettes, these meals are restaurant-worthy in flavor but wildly easy to make at home. I'll be dipping back into this book again and again, in every season."

SARAH COPELAND, CREATOR OF *EDIBLE LIVING* AND AUTHOR OF *FEAST, EVERY DAY IS SATURDAY*, AND *INSTANT FAMILY MEALS*

"Trust Susan Spungen and follow her lead. *Veg Forward* is glorious—fresh, colorful, smart, and perfectly seasonal. Susan's food always makes me happy."

DAVID TANIS, CHEF AND AUTHOR

To Amita & Sunish
Keep on Vegging!

VEG
FORWARD

Super-Delicious Recipes that Put Produce at
the Center of Your Plate

SUSAN SPUNGEN

HARPER
Celebrate

Published by Harper Celebrate, an imprint of HarperCollins Focus LLC.

Photography © Susan Spungen.

Author portraits by Tara Sgroi (pages 8, 10, 11, and 246).

Design by Cybele Grandjean.

ISBN: 978-0-7852-9299-9 (epub)
ISBN: 978-0-7852-9298-2 (HC)

Printed in Malaysia

23 24 25 26 27 OFF 6 5 4 3 2

To Steve, my partner in the fields and in life.
May we continue to grow together.

VEG FORWARD

CONTENTS

INTRODUCTION

This is a vegetable book for everyone.

Not just vegetarians, but anyone who loves vegetables or *wants to* love vegetables. You know they're good for you. Good for the planet. Good for your pocketbook. And they're just, well, *good*, providing that you know what to do with them.

Whether you get your vegetables from a CSA (ours is the pick-your-own kind), a farmers' market, a farmstand, a backyard garden, or the supermarket, I want this book to inspire you to cook them in new and delicious ways that bring them to the center of your plate. The veggies in these recipes are driving the bus; they're not just along for the ride. Every idea for every recipe puts the vegetables first. They are never just tacked on as an afterthought. They are the "meat" of the meal.

I didn't set out to create a book that was completely vegetarian—just vegetable *forward*—but the more I concentrated on the vegetables themselves, the less need I saw for meat. You'll find plenty of ideas for that fennel bulb that you brought home from the market—or that brought itself home in your CSA box (the Sheet-Pan Braised Fennel with Parm and Hazelnuts on page 197, perhaps). Or maybe you were wondering what to do with those curly green garlic scapes you see everywhere in the spring. Sure, you could make a centerpiece for your table with them. But better yet, why not make the best garlic bread you've ever had with Garlic Scape Pesto (page 23)? Or maybe you're bored with the same old zucchini recipes. I've got some good ones for you, including Grilled Zucchini with Whipped Ricotta, Calabrian Chili, and Almonds (page 111), or a decadent chocolate zucchini loaf (page 117). I leave no tomato unturned in the summer chapter (page 49) with tons of ways to eat them fresh, cooked, or preserved for later (page 216).

As you explore, you might learn about some new varieties you haven't cooked with before, like almost-seedless Jimmy Nardello peppers with their sweet, nutty flavor for Farro and Sweet Red Pepper Bake (page 55), or crunchy and striking Tardivo radicchio for a sharp and satisfying winter salad with good looks to spare (page 195). I'll have you on the lookout for Sungold tomatoes, those little orbs that are the color of a clementine and nearly as sweet.

Because of seasonal and regional variations in what's available, I'll give you lots of ideas for substitutions, so you can make many of the recipes most of the time, not just on a dewy day in June. While it's fun to eat and shop in a hyper-seasonal way, that isn't always possible, even for me. Zucchini, Leek, and Potato Soup (page 21) is the recipe I have made the most in this book, and it can be cooked at any time of year with supermarket ingredients.

While you'll find plenty of ideas for those times when the parade of produce is nonstop—from May to November, at least in these parts—I'll also show you how to make the most of the supermarket vegetable aisle in the dark days of winter. (Check out the Onion and Cabbage Panade on page 181, a comforting dish that's like the best part of French onion soup.) You'll find plenty of ideas to inspire you, no matter the season. Refreshing soups for muggy days when all you can manage is to run the blender. Warm-weather grain bowls. Big platter salads. Fruit snacking cakes.

Since it's vegetables we're talking about, I've organized this book seasonally. But there is a huge amount of variation in what's available in the markets, and many vegetables—lettuce and other tender greens, broccoli, kohlrabi, and radishes, for instance—appear in both spring and fall. Accordingly, you'll find recipes for the same vegetables in more than one chapter, like an autumnal recipe for Poblano Corn Chowder (page 153) in the fall chapter, as well as a grilled Smoky Corn Salad (page 107) that's perfect for August in the summer chapter. As one season slowly morphs into the next, some vegetables phase in, others phase out, and others stay around for months. The seasons will be different for you if you live in California or Alaska, which is why I've included a handy index in the back of the book where you can look up the vegetables you want to cook and find the recipes that use them.

I BRAKE FOR ZUCCHINI

Despite my lifelong passion for produce, I've never been a vegetarian. You'll find recipes with a little sausage (End of Summer Vegetable Soup, page 89), occasionally a little shrimp (like in the Okonomiyaki on page 185), and a little bacon or soppressata, but all these can be easily left out.

We've come a long way from the canned and frozen vegetables of my youth (though to my mother's credit, we did eat plenty of fresh vegetables, including a salad at every meal). I remember her excitement and sense of triumph when we screeched to a halt at a roadside stand where she snagged a giant zucchini for a nickel on the way home from a day at the Jersey shore. This gave me an early appreciation of the pleasures of produce. I brake for zucchini too. These days, there's hardly a big city or small town without a thriving farmers' market. I think of them as our modern-day village greens. At my local market, the Union Square Greenmarket in New York City, random strangers quite often ask me what to do with a particular vegetable when they see me confidently choosing my loot. It can take me hours to shop because I run into so many friends and acquaintances. Like many people, I get so much more than produce there: I feel *connected*.

In writing this book, my goal was to create recipes that coax a maximum amount of flavor from a minimum number of ingredients. This is food that tastes as good as it looks and looks as good as it tastes. Every ingredient in every recipe has a purpose, and if the ingredient didn't add something important, I left it out. There is nothing superfluous. Now, come veg forward with me.

ABOUT THE RECIPES

A recipe is a guide, not a god. I believe in recipes, but I also believe in your intuition, and I encourage you to use it. In many recipes, I don't give you exact amounts of salt and pepper, except when they are cooked into a dish and it matters. If you're roasting a vegetable, I *trust* you to lightly sprinkle it with salt and turn a peppermill a few times to season. If it's not enough, you can always add more later.

For these recipes, which involve plants, there is so much variation in the size and qualities of each ingredient that you will be forced to use your judgment to get the best results. For example, my bunch of kale might be twice (or half) as big as yours, so wherever possible and where it matters most, I offer at least two, and maybe three, measurements: the weight of the produce, the volume (in cups) once it's prepped, and how many vegetables to buy.

Another way that fresh produce can vary is in its moisture content. The fresher something is, the higher the moisture content, and the faster it will cook. I want you to pay attention to all these variables and learn to use your gut instincts.

A NOTE ABOUT THE PHOTOGRAPHS

I photographed this entire book on an iPhone. That's because I wanted the book to be authentically diaristic. I wanted to be able to shoot ingredients and recipes in the moment, rather than photographing everything in a grueling ten-day session as is done with most cookbooks. I knew there was no way that every vegetable would be available in that short period of time and certainly not as their best selves.

Case in point: One August evening, I sliced into a big heirloom tomato for dinner. It was so beautiful inside that I took a quick photo of it then and there. I later tried to best that shot by buying a slew of heirlooms and slicing into each. Guess what? None were as good as the one that became our dinner that night. You can see the winning tomato on page 91. I hope these photos inspire you to make every recipe.

VEG FORWARD

VEG FORWARD

THE VEG FORWARD KITCHEN: A SHORT, OPINIONATED GUIDE

The following are my MVPs that will shake up your veg kitchen, give vegetable-rich meals deeper flavor, and take your cooking in new and unexpected directions.

THE PANTRY

These pantry ingredients will elevate your cooking.

Balsamic vinegar

Keep a bottle of the good stuff around for balancing the bitterness of radicchio or other bitter greens. Unfortunately, balsamic got a bad name from the watered-down, caramel-colored supermarket imitations. Although you don't need to pay $50 or more for a bottle of the good syrupy stuff that's aged in a series of oak barrels, it's worth investing in a decent one. I like Giuseppe Giusti from Italy, which is aged for twelve years, or Elsa, which comes in six- and twelve-year versions, and are priced accordingly. All are available on Amazon for about $25 and $40 dollars, respectively.

Dried cranberry beans

Also called Roman beans or borlotti beans, cranberry beans are the best all-around dried bean, in my humble opinion. Mottled with pink streaks when raw, they turn a slightly purple-pink color when cooked. They have a creamy quality but still hold their shape thanks to their thicker skin, making them perfect for salads and soups. They're widely available (at your supermarket, find them under the name Roman beans) or from ranchogordo.com or Kalustyan's (foodsofnations.com).

Pearled farro

A versatile high-protein, high-fiber variety of ancient wheat, farro is now available in most supermarkets—thank goodness! It's easy to cook (it takes just 15 to 20 minutes), after which it retains some springy chew. I like to use it in salads, pilafs, bakes, and soups.

Freekeh

This smoked green durum wheat is set on fire to burn the straw and chaff. Since the grains are still young and moist, they don't burn, but they do take on a whiff of smoky flavor as they roast. This is another 20-minute variety and a nice alternative to everyday grains, like bulgur—which it is similar to, with a unique flavor. Be sure to get cracked (not whole-grain) freekeh. You may have to order this online, and you can find it at (foodsofnations.com and amazon.com).

Lentils

Green (Puy) lentils and beluga lentils are my go-to for salads and soups because they hold their shape better than brown lentils, which get mushy and have a chalkiness that some people object to. Small green lentils are more widely available in stores than belugas, which are smaller, darker, and firmer and look a bit like black caviar. They cook in about 20 minutes. Order them from Kalustyan's (foodsofnations.com), nuts.com, or amazon.com.

Dried porcini mushrooms

I use these often to add a deep, earthy, shroomy flavor. They're usually sold in one-ounce bags, often in the produce section of the supermarket, but because I use a lot of them and they last a long time, I get bigger bags from Kalustyan's (foodsofnations.com) and keep them in my pantry.

Nori

These dried seaweed sheets are in most supermarkets (look in the Asian section) and they last forever. I always keep a box on hand. Nori snacks are in many supermarkets and work fine as a flavor component (though not for rolling sushi) if your store doesn't have sheets.

Quinoa

Though we treat it like a grain, quinoa is actually a seed from a plant of the amaranth family. It's higher in protein than other grains, making it a great choice for vegetarians. Its fluffy qualities make it excellent as a filling or in a salad. You'll find it in rainbow varieties (with white, red, and black), or all white or all red (which is actually a reddish brown). I like to use the red variety in certain recipes for its color; however, they all taste about the same.

Raw sugar

I use minimally processed raw coarse sugar to finish many of my baked goods and fruit desserts because I like the color and the crunch. Some recipes insist on Demerara, which is hard to find. But guess what? There's no discernible difference between Demerara and turbinado sugar, which is sold in every supermarket as Sugar in the Raw, so I use that.

THE SPICE CABINET

Don't store your dry spices above your stove—the heat will kill their flavor.

Aleppo-style pepper

Considered a "semi-dry" pepper, it's ground into a coarse powder from the Halaby pepper and is named for the city in Syria from which it originally hails. It has a fruity flavor and can be used liberally without making things too spicy. Morton & Bassett is the supermarket brand to look for, or you can order it from Burlap & Barrel (burlapandbarrel.com), where it goes by the name of Silk Chili.

Smoked chili flakes

These are milder than typical red pepper flakes, so you can sprinkle them liberally. They bring a hint of smoke and heat to everything they touch. I can't live without them and order them from Daphnis and Chloe (daphnisandchloe.com).

Roasted cumin

Nothing can compare to toasting cumin seeds in a hot pan and grinding them yourself, but the roasted cumin available in the supermarket spice rack comes close.

Garlic powder

I used to be a snob about garlic powder, but I've since realized that it adds a savory flavor to things that would otherwise be difficult to infuse with garlic. I love sprinkling it on asparagus and other vegetables like cauliflower, or tofu before roasting.

Maldon salt

This is a British flaky sea salt that comes in delicate crystals that are easily crumbled between the fingers, unlike some other sea salts that come in larger, harder crystals. There are few dishes that don't benefit from a final sprinkle of this salt.

Dried oregano

This is the only herb I prefer dried to fresh. It's superior to fresh oregano, which can be strong and bitter. If possible, get the kind that's still on the stem in bushy branches. Crumbling it fresh releases its sweet and fragrant flavor. Look for it in Italian specialty stores or get it from daphnisandchloe.com.

Smoked paprika

I almost never use regular paprika anymore because I prefer the subtle smokiness that this variety brings. The supermarket version is fine.

Sumac

This is a beautiful deep red, almost purple, powdery spice made from the dried and ground berries of the sumac shrub. You've likely had it on that plate of hummus at a Middle Eastern restaurant. (Maybe you thought it was paprika.) It has a powerful powdered lemon flavor—a light sprinkle will add a hint of fruity acidity to whatever it graces. Look for it on your supermarket shelves, where it's making more frequent appearances, or order from diaspora.com, burlapandbarrel.com, or amazon.com, where many brands are available.

THE FRIDGE DOOR

When I'm looking for inspiration, or am trying to balance a dish, this is where flavor lives.

Calabrian chili paste

These small red chilies come whole and packed in oil, but I prefer the paste form because it's easier to use. I like the Tutto Calabria brand. It's slightly fermented, so it has an underlying funk. It has a scalp-tingling—not mouth-burning—heat. If you don't find this in your supermarket, you'll find the best prices on Amazon or at Trader Joe's, sold under the name Bomba Sauce.

Chili crisp

This versatile condiment is now the number one condiment in China, thanks to the introduction in 1996 of the mother of all chili crisps, Lao Gan Ma. Chili crisp adds heat and texture and should be used mostly as a finishing condiment. It usually consists of chilies fried in oil, along with garlic and sometimes shallots, but there is an infinite number of variations. I keep a hot and a milder one around. For the mild, I like S & B Umami topping with crunchy garlic. You might think its crunchy bits are garlic slices, but they're sliced almonds. Its deliciousness may be heightened by the MSG in it. Fly by Jing, my favorite spicy one, contains no MSG but gets its umami from black garlic and fermented black beans. Google it. You'll find a multitude of brands from different sources.

Chili garlic sauce

This is a good all-purpose condiment to turn up the heat, and the addition of garlic can save a step when seasoning. It comes in one of those little plastic jars with the green lids you'll find in the Asian section of your supermarket. It's similar to sambal oelek (which is spicier and has no garlic), and sriracha (which has sugar and is milder). All are made by Huy Fong Foods.

Harissa

The North African red pepper sauce and paste has become as common as ketchup in the United States and is used as a condiment and in sauces in some of the same ways. There are many different brands and varieties out there, and they vary in flavor, heat level, and consistency. One of my favorites, Mina Harissa—which is a loose sauce, not a paste—comes in mild and hot varieties (I prefer mild), and can be ordered (try Amazon or Walmart), or found on a supermarket shelf. I also like the one from New York Shuk (nyshuk.com).

Miso

Whether you're making an instant soup or slipping it into dressings and sauces, miso brings umami to everything you use it in. Sweet white miso is the one I use. It's available in most supermarkets.

Mustards

Different vinaigrettes require different mustards. Whole grain is useful when you want a little texture and pops of flavor. Dijon is good for most everything. My favorite brand is Maille, available in many grocery stores in several varieties. Use Rich Country Dijon when you want a creamier, milder flavor (it has a hint of oil in it, which smooths out the flavor), and Honey Dijon when you need to balance an overly sharp dressing.

Olives

My go-to olives are green Castelvetrano for their mild, creamy, not-too-salty flavor, and black oil-cured olives for their fruity, buttery concentrated flavor. I also appreciate how easy oil-cured olives are to pit when I'm in a hurry. The oil-cured ones are usually found in the refrigerated deli section of the supermarket or on the olive bar. Kalamata olives are good for Greek and other salads.

Ponzu

Similar to soy sauce or tamari (which it contains), ponzu has a high percentage of citrus, especially yuzu, which is a flavor that is otherwise difficult or impossible to obtain.

Fresh ricotta

Many supermarkets and cheese shops carry what is known as "fresh" ricotta, usually in the cheese department. Often it's sold in a metal can with drainage holes poked in the bottom with a bulging top, the whole thing wrapped in plastic. Or it might also be packaged by the store into smaller containers or sold in bulk. This fluffy, creamy, pure white cheese tastes like fresh, sweet milk and is far superior to the mass-produced packaged versions you'll find in the dairy section of your store.

Stock concentrates

I've stopped buying boxed stocks, because they're expensive, watery tasting, take up too much room, and I end up throwing out half the carton because it lingered too long in the back of the fridge. Now I keep squeeze bottles of Kitchen Accomplice chicken or veggie broth, as well as Better Than Bouillon, also in chicken and vegetable varieties. They add a lot of flavor but are somewhat salty, so go easy. Both brands are available in supermarkets, with Kitchen Accomplice being a little trickier to find. You can order it from morethangourmet.com or amazon.com.

Tahini

It can be hard to find high-quality brands on supermarket shelves, so it's worth ordering online. My favorite is Seed & Mill (seedandmill.com). It's delicious enough to eat right out of the jar.

Yondu

You probably won't find this in your supermarket, but you can order it on Amazon. It's a liquid umami seasoning sometimes referred to as vegan fish sauce because it can be used in much the same way. It's made from fermented soybeans and vegetable stock. A little goes a long way, and it should be used instead of salt (or at least before using salt). It does wonders for tahini sauce. I also use a dash in soups, stews, and noodle dishes when I'm balancing flavors at the end.

THE HERB GARDEN

Nothing adds more flavor, freshness, and beauty to your cooking than fresh herbs. And nothing saves more money and prevents more waste than growing your own. Basil (several varieties and colors), parsley, thyme, tarragon, chives, shiso, rosemary, and sage can all be grown in pots on a windowsill, balcony, urban fire escape, or deck. Herbs are easy to grow (even for a beginner gardener!) and will beautify your space.

VEG ARTILLERY

Prep Gear
Knives

If you're cooking with vegetables, you're going to be doing a lot of chopping. Dull knives are more dangerous than sharp ones, because the possibility of the knife slipping while you're cutting an onion or a butternut squash is far greater. I am brand agnostic and have a mix in my knife drawer, but they are all fully forged, rather than stamped, making them harder, heavier, and more durable. Most importantly, they will hold their edge longer. A forged knife will also feel heavier and more balanced in your hand.

Keeping your knives sharp is important. There's an art to it (which you can easily teach yourself with online

videos), and it requires only a whetstone. You can also have a professional do the same for you, if you know someone. Even a locksmith can sharpen your knives since they use the same equipment to smooth out keys. Beware of doing this too often though, since a fair amount of metal is removed each time, and eventually the shape of your blade can change and may no longer make good contact with your cutting surface. In between sharpenings, use a honing steel to maintain and restore the edge.

Cutting boards

It's important to have an ample cutting board to prep on. I prefer a large end-grain wooden board to contain whatever I'm working on. A good wooden board is superior in every way. It's gentler on your knives, it feels more stable, and it even makes a nicer sound when chopping. I have plastic boards too and use them when handling meat or fish so that I can clean them more easily or run them through the dishwasher. One of the most basic things I learned from working in professional kitchens is to work from left to right. Pile whatever you're prepping on the left side of your board and move the item to the right as you cut, transferring it to a bowl or baking sheet if needed. (Reverse the direction if you are left-handed.) This basic organization is critical for speed and efficiency.

Mandoline

This is the most important tool I want you to have. My preference is the Kyocera with an adjustable ceramic blade because it's easy to use and easy to store, as it fits in a drawer (keep it on its side with the blade against the side to prevent any accidental cuts). It's super handy for thinly slicing vegetables, and for shaving radishes or fennel on top of salads and other dishes for a pretty finishing touch. It's also great for hard cheeses like Parmesan. Since it's less than $20, I don't feel bad if I need a new one every few years.

Cut-proof gloves

I've seen too many people (including myself) get a quick and nasty cut from a mandoline. I always wear one of these gloves if my hand is going to be anywhere near the blade. Don't get the mandoline without getting the glove! They're very inexpensive and abundant online. Google it!

Food processor

There really is nothing else that whizzes ingredients together like a food processor does. I like having both a full-size machine and a mini version. The slicing blade quickly shreds kale or Brussels sprouts, and the grating blade dispatches large amounts of cheese or raw beets or carrots. The mini version, which can be tucked away in a drawer or cabinet, does a good job of chopping without completely pulverizing ingredients like garlic or parsley when you're feeling lazy. The mini size is also perfect for small batches of pesto or grinding nuts or sesame seeds.

Box grater

For raw grated vegetables in salads, a box grater gives a better texture than a food processor. It creates a finer, more delicate shred than the machine, which makes raw vegetables for salads a bit easier to chew. It's great for those times when you just need a small amount of something and you don't want to get the food processor dirty.

High-speed blender

The best (and priciest) is the Vitamix. Its powerful motor makes short work of blending almost anything into a velvety smooth puree. A refurbished one will cost you less money, as will a Ninja or a Blendtec.

Salad spinner

I'm always a little shocked when I go to someone else's home and discover they don't have a salad spinner. I use mine at least several times a week. I also have a mini one for herbs, which can also be used for storage of said herbs. My favorite is from Oxo. They come in several sizes.

Cooking Gear
Baking sheets

Professional sheet pans are sturdier, larger, and conduct heat better than the flimsy ones you'll find in a supermarket. They will also last forever. These roughly 11-by-17-inch pans with a raised, rolled edge are indispensable. They won't warp and pop out of shape in the oven and are perfect for everything from roasting vegetables to baking galettes to being placed underneath a potentially drippy baking dish full of lasagna. I use them constantly for everything. Ideally you should have at least two. If you can buy them from a restaurant supply store, they will be well-priced and lacking unnecessary bells and whistles like a textured surface. I am also a fan of quarter sheet pans (about 9 by 13 inches), which are handy for so many things, such as toasting nuts, baking sweet potatoes, or cooking a smaller amount of anything.

Dutch oven

A good all-purpose size is a 5.5 quart (26 cm). Enameled cast-iron is best, and they are usually marked with a number on the bottom that tells you the diameter in centimeters. They can be pricey, so if you can't afford a new one, look for used ones in thrift shops and flea markets. Because of their nonreactive surface, you can cook, store, reheat, and serve all in the same pot. These are good for simmering soups and for serving foods you want to stay warm (like mashed potatoes), and are pretty enough to bring to the table.

Skillets

I use heavy, hard-anodized, nonstick skillets from Anolon or Calphalon for most of my cooking. I especially recommend a large (12-inch) one. It gets the most use in my kitchen, because when I sauté (especially mushrooms), I don't want to crowd the food. I also have cast-iron skillets in various sizes; 10-inch is a good all-purpose size. My favorite belonged to my grandmother, and others I have bought at yard sales.

Grill platter and basket (aka grill wok)

These accessories are especially well-suited to cooking veggies on the grill. The flat design of the grill platter (from Weber) has perforations that allow the heat of the grill to get to the vegetables, like asparagus, without letting anything fall through. A grill basket, sometimes called a grill wok, looks like a round or square metal bowl with holes in it. It's great for small things like mushrooms, sliced onions, broccoli, cauliflower, or string beans. Because you'll pile the veggies up in these baskets, there won't be as much direct heat and

the vegetables can also steam a bit, which is what you want when you're grilling mushrooms, broccoli, cauliflower, or string beans. You can easily toss the items as though you were cooking on the stovetop.

And Five Surprisingly Useful Tools
Bench scraper

Besides helping you lift a dough that's sticking, it's super handy for scraping your work surface to clean it, for transferring piles of vegetables to the pot, cutting gnocchi, and about a million other things.

Ice cream scoop

This is the best tool for scraping and scooping the seeds out of winter squash. I like the old-fashioned click scoop with a somewhat sharp edge.

Melon baller

This is handy for removing the seeds of certain vegetables, like cucumbers, or coring apples once they've been cut in half—but not for making melon balls.

KitchenAid pasta attachment

If you have a stand mixer already, check out the space-saving attachments that you can get for your machine before investing in a whole new appliance. The strong motor of a KitchenAid can power a number of other jobs, including pasta. If you've never made homemade pasta before, I implore you to try it. It's a magical process and one that takes the lasagna recipe on page 175 from excellent to over-the-top good. And the machine is fast, since you can crank it up to a fairly high speed.

Tortilla press

Who doesn't love tacos? I'm hoping to convince you to make homemade tortillas (see page 214), and you'll need a tortilla press to do it. They range from very basic and inexpensive ($15 or $20) to a little fancier. I have my eye on the one from Masienda ($95) for its ease of use. It comes in three stylish powder-coated hues.

VEG FORWARD

SPRING

SPRING

VEG FORWARD

MAKES 2 (12-INCH) PIZZAS

ASPARAGUS PIZZA WITH ARUGULA SALAD

A cool, acidic salad piled onto a hot pizza is one of the best things in life. The contrast of the hot cheese and crust wrapped around the salad, which wilts just a little, is so satisfying (yes, you have permission to fold your slice). I like to buy bunches of arugula with larger leaves when I see them, but any size will work.

For the pizza

1 recipe pizza dough (page 211), left at room temperature for 1 hour if previously chilled

All-purpose flour, for handling the dough

3 teaspoons olive oil, divided, plus more for brushing

1 cup ricotta, preferably fresh, or 6 ounces soft goat cheese (or a combination)

6 ounces fresh mozzarella, torn into pieces

28 asparagus (1 1/2 bunches), trimmed and halved lengthwise unless pencil-thin

1 jalapeño, thinly sliced

Kosher salt and freshly ground pepper

For the salad

3 cups arugula

12 Castelvetrano olives (about 1/2 cup) or other green olives, pitted and halved

1 tablespoon lemon juice

2 teaspoons olive oil

Kosher salt and freshly ground pepper

Instructions

1. Heat the oven to 500°F, or the highest setting, with a baking steel or stone inside on the center rack. Heat for 45 minutes.

2. **To make the pizza:** Scrape the dough out of the bowl onto a generously floured surface. Divide into 2 equal pieces using a bench scraper, handling the dough as little as possible. Cut a 12-inch sheet of parchment, spray or brush with olive oil, and place on a pizza peel or the back of a rimmed baking sheet or cookie sheet.

3. Transfer one piece of dough to the parchment and, with floured hands, gently stretch into a rough 12-inch circle. Top with dollops of half the ricotta or crumbles of half the goat cheese, and half the mozzarella, scattering evenly.

4. Toss half the asparagus and the jalapeño with 1 teaspoon of the oil to coat, and lightly season with salt and pepper. Scatter the vegetable mixture on the pizza, drizzle with 1 teaspoon olive oil, and slide the pizza, still on the parchment, onto the steel, stone, or heated baking sheet.

5. Bake for 10 to 12 minutes, until the crust is well browned on the edges and the cheese is bubbling. Use the peel to scoop up the pizza, giving a little tug on the paper to help if needed, and transfer to a serving board.

6. Repeat the steps with the remaining dough and ingredients to make a second pizza.

7. **To make the salad:** Toss the arugula with the olives, lemon juice, olive oil, salt, and pepper.

8. Top each pizza with half the salad and serve immediately.

If you don't have a baking steel or stone, use a baking sheet and heat it, upside down, on the center rack for at least 15 minutes.

If you want to make only one pizza, freeze the other round of dough to use another time. Defrost overnight in the fridge before using.

VEG FORWARD

3

VEG FORWARD

SERVES 4

WARM-WEATHER FARRO BOWLS WITH GRILLED TOFU

My ideal grain bowl, which is in regular rotation in our house, is a combination of warm and cold, cooked and raw, with crispy, creamy, and crunchy elements. It goes light on the chewy, nutty farro and heavy on the vegetables—asparagus, sugar snaps, fennel, and cherry tomatoes. Grilling heightens their flavors, but everything can be done in the oven too.

For the farro

1 teaspoon kosher salt

2 tablespoons apple cider vinegar

1 cup uncooked pearled farro

For the tofu

1 package extra-firm tofu

¼ cup of your favorite barbecue sauce

2 teaspoons smoked paprika

2 teaspoons garlic powder

½ teaspoon kosher salt

For the vegetables

1 cup sugar snap peas, strings removed

½ bulb fennel

20 pencil asparagus, trimmed

Olive oil

Kosher salt and freshly ground pepper

1 pint grape or cherry tomatoes, halved

Charred Tomato Vinaigrette (page 225)

2 to 4 scallions or spring onions, thinly sliced

1 watermelon radish or 2 regular red radishes, thinly sliced

Fresh herbs (optional)

Instructions

1. **To cook the farro:** Bring a large saucepan of water to a boil and add the salt and vinegar. Add the farro and return to a boil. Reduce to a strong simmer and cook for 18 to 20 minutes until the grains start to split and they are al dente. Drain the farro and spread out on a dinner plate to cool. Set aside.

2. **To prep the tofu:** Cut the tofu into 4 thick slabs and cut each slab in half. Lay out between a few layers of paper towels and press lightly to absorb the excess moisture. Transfer to a plate and coat with the barbecue sauce on all sides. Mix the paprika, garlic powder, and salt together and spread out on a small plate. Dip the two largest sides of each piece of tofu in the spice mixture to coat and return to a clean, dry plate.

3. **To prep and grill the vegetables:** Blanch the snap peas for about 10 seconds and refresh in ice water. Pat dry and cut into slivers. Shave the fennel as thinly as possible, using a mandoline slicer, if you have one, or a sharp knife. Set aside.

4. Light a gas grill to medium-high. Heat a grill platter (see page 29) on a grill set to high heat. Toss the asparagus with enough oil to lightly coat them and season with salt and pepper. Spread the asparagus on one side of the grill platter. Cook the asparagus, tossing once with tongs, for about 5 minutes, or until browned in spots. Transfer to a plate and set aside. Set the grill platter aside.

5. Oil the grill grates with a pair of tongs and a paper towel soaked with oil and place the tofu on the grill. Cook the tofu for about 3 minutes per side until lightly charred and transfer back to the plate.

6. **To assemble the bowls:** Divide the farro among four wide, shallow bowls. Arrange the asparagus, snap peas, fennel, tomatoes, and tofu on top of the farro. Spoon some of the dressing on each bowl. Garnish with the scallions, radishes, and herbs (if using) and serve any additional dressing on the side.

If you don't have a grill, everything can be done in the oven instead. Roast the asparagus, tomatoes, and tofu at 425°F, all on the same baking sheet.

Try the Green Tahini-Yogurt "Everything Sauce" (page 220) and/or Salsa Macha (page 214) to change up the flavors.

Use this as a template to create your own bowl for any season. Brown rice, freekeh, and quinoa all work well.

VEG FORWARD

SERVES 4

BUCATINI WITH PEA PESTO, RICOTTA, AND SHAVED ASPARAGUS

This simple yet satisfying pasta dish requires no cooking (aside from the pasta), making it quick to throw together. The thinly shaved asparagus soften from the heat of the pasta, turning them into supple, satiny ribbons.

Ingredients

1 cup fresh or thawed frozen peas

1 garlic clove

1/2 cup grated pecorino or Parmesan (1/2 ounce)

1/2 loosely packed cup herbs, such as mint, basil, or parsley

1/4 cup extra-virgin olive oil

1/2 teaspoon kosher salt

Freshly ground pepper

8 ounces bucatini

1 lemon

1 cup ricotta, preferably fresh

8 ounces asparagus, shaved with a vegetable peeler

Red pepper flakes

Instructions

1. Combine the peas, garlic, cheese, herbs, oil, salt, and pepper in a food processor. Pulse to a coarse puree.

2. Cook the pasta in well-salted water until al dente.

3. Scoop out 1 cup of pasta water and drain the pasta.

4. Return the pasta to the pot and toss with the pea pesto. Loosen with some pasta water. Season with salt and pepper to taste.

5. Divide among four bowls and grate lemon zest over the bowls. Squeeze the lemon over each serving.

6. Dollop the ricotta over each serving and top with the asparagus.

7. Sprinkle with red pepper flakes.

You can use thick spaghetti instead of bucatini.

VEG FORWARD

7

SERVES 4 AS A LIGHT MEAL OR 4 TO 6 AS A SIDE

ROASTED ASPARAGUS WITH WHITE BEANS AND GREEN GARLIC PESTO

This simple assemblage makes a filling vegetarian lunch or a side dish for dinner. Green garlic, a.k.a. spring garlic or young garlic, is just that—garlic that hasn't fully matured. Because of its burgeoning popularity, many farmers grow it as a separate crop so there's more to sell. Its milder but still garlicky flavor is perfect in pesto. This recipe makes more pesto than you will need here, but it will keep well in the fridge.

For the pesto

2 to 3 thick stalks green garlic, trimmed and sliced into 1/4-inch rounds (about 2/3 cup)

1 cup loosely packed Italian parsley leaves

1 cup loosely packed mint leaves

2 cups loosely packed arugula

2 ounces (about 2/3 cup) walnuts

1 ounce grated pecorino (3/4 fluffy cup)

1/2 teaspoon salt, plus more to taste

3/4 cup extra-virgin olive oil

Pinch of red pepper flakes

Freshly ground pepper

For the asparagus

1 pound (about 1 bunch) asparagus

2 teaspoons olive oil

Kosher salt and freshly ground pepper

1 (15.5-ounce) can butter beans or cannellini beans, drained and rinsed

1 tablespoon lemon juice

Chive flowers for garnish (optional)

Instructions

1. **To make the pesto:** Put the green garlic, parsley, mint, and arugula in a food processor and pulse until everything is coarsely chopped. Scrape down the sides of the food processor. Add the walnuts, pecorino, salt, olive oil, red pepper flakes, and freshly ground pepper, and pulse again just until nuts are chopped, and everything is combined. Season with salt and pepper to taste, and add more oil if you want a thinner texture (or add more oil as you use the pesto if needed). Set aside. The pesto can be refrigerated, covered by a thin slick of olive oil, for a week or two, or frozen for up to 3 months, perhaps portioned out into ice cube trays.

2. **To make the asparagus:** Snap the tough bottoms off the asparagus spears, and peel the bottoms of the thicker stalks, if desired. Toss with the oil and sprinkle lightly with salt and pepper. Heat the oven to 500°F, or the highest setting, with a baking sheet in the upper middle rack. Carefully remove the hot baking sheet and spread the asparagus on the pan. Roast until tender and browned, 12 to 14 minutes, tossing halfway through the cooking.

3. Toss the beans with 1/4 cup of the pesto, the lemon juice, and more oil if needed. Adjust the seasonings.

4. Spread the beans out on a serving platter and top with the asparagus. Garnish with chive flowers (if using).

To grill the asparagus, heat a grill platter (see page 29) or a double thickness of heavy-duty foil with some holes punched in it on a grill set to high heat to preheat. Reduce to medium-high and spread the asparagus out on the grill platter or foil. Cook for 2 to 3 minutes, until lightly charred, and turn. Cook for another 2 to 3 minutes. The time will depend on the thickness of the spears. Remove from the grill and set aside.

There are so many other ways to use this pesto: melt it into a simple pasta dish, put a spoonful in soup, spread it on toast as is or topped with ricotta, or dollop it on pizza.

VEG FORWARD

9

VEG FORWARD

SERVES 4 TO 6

PAN-ROASTED ARTICHOKE FRITTATA WITH MINT AND LEMON

This artichoke frittata is an homage to an utterly delicious and simple marriage of artichokes and eggs that I once tasted at Sostanza, a charming trattoria in Florence (you should go there). Since artichokes require a bit of work to clean, this is a good way to stretch a smaller number of artichokes to feed six people.

Ingredients

1 lemon

1 ½ pounds baby artichokes (12 to 14, depending on size)

2 tablespoons olive oil

A few sprigs of thyme

1 ¼ teaspoons kosher salt, divided

Freshly ground pepper

2 to 3 garlic cloves, minced, or 1 tablespoon Big Batch Roasted Garlic (page 217), or 3 stalks green garlic, thinly sliced

2 tablespoons dry white wine

6 large eggs

½ cup milk or heavy cream

½ fluffy cup grated Parmesan (½ ounce)

1 tablespoon unsalted butter

½ fluffy cup grated Gruyère (½ ounce)

Fresh mint leaves for serving

Lemon wedges for serving

Instructions

1. Cut the lemon in half and squeeze the juice into a medium bowl half-filled with water. Add the lemon halves to the water.

2. Cut off the top ½ inch of an artichoke and trim the bottom of the stem. Snap off the tough, darker green outer leaves. Keep going until you get to the palest green, almost yellow, leaves. Pare the bottom and stem smooth with a paring knife. Cut in half lengthwise, and if there is any sign of a fuzzy choke, scoop it out with a melon baller or paring knife. Place in the lemon water and repeat with the remaining artichokes.

3. Heat the oven to 350°F. Add the oil to a medium 10-inch nonstick skillet with an ovenproof handle, along with ½ cup of the lemon water, the artichokes, thyme, ¾ teaspoon of the salt, and pepper. Bring to a simmer, and cook, covered, over medium-low heat until tender, tossing occasionally, 10 to 12 minutes.

4. Remove the lid, turn the heat up to medium-high, and cook for 8 to 10 minutes, tossing occasionally, until golden brown on both sides. Add the garlic after 5 minutes, tossing until golden. Be careful it doesn't burn. Pour in the wine, stirring to loosen any brown bits. Cook until evaporated, about 1 minute. Transfer the artichokes to a plate and rinse out the skillet. Discard the thyme.

5. In a medium bowl, whisk the eggs with the milk or cream, Parmesan, the remaining ½ teaspoon salt, and pepper. Heat the same skillet over medium heat and add the butter. Swirl until melted and add the egg mixture, followed by the artichokes. Pull the edges of the egg back with a rubber spatula, letting the liquid flow to the edges until the eggs are somewhat set throughout (the edges should be set, but the middle should be runny with cooked curds). Redistribute the artichokes if necessary. Sprinkle with the Gruyère and transfer to the oven. Cook until just set in the center, about 10 minutes. Broil the top for 2 to 3 minutes to brown, if desired. Slide onto a serving plate. Serve warm or at room temperature with fresh mint leaves and lemon wedges.

The pan-roasted artichokes are delicious on their own. If you want to serve them that way, you're done at the end of step four. Sprinkle some fresh mint and squeeze some lemon over top of them and eat them with your fingers.

SERVES 4

EMERALD PASTA WITH NETTLE SAUCE

Whether you find them in the farmers' market or your own backyard, nettles are one of spring's earliest greens. They have a mild flavor most similar to spinach, and they're an easy foraging project.

Ingredients

8 ounces pasta with deep grooves, such as fusilloni giganti, fusilli corti bucati, or gemelli

1/4 cup grated Parmesan cheese, plus more for serving

2 tablespoons unsalted butter, softened

Kosher salt and freshly ground pepper

For the nettle sauce

2 tablespoons olive oil

4 to 6 garlic cloves, sliced

2 cups cooked nettles (see below)

2 tablespoons snipped chives

Grated zest of 1 lemon

Pinch of red pepper flakes

3/4 cup hot water or vegetable stock (page 226), divided

Kosher salt and freshly ground pepper

Instructions

1. Cook the pasta in a large pot of boiling salted water until al dente. Scoop out and set aside 1 cup of the pasta water. Drain the pasta.

2. **For the sauce:** Warm the oil in a small skillet and add the garlic. Cook over medium heat (reduce to medium-low if the garlic is browning too quickly) until the garlic looks toasty brown all over, 5 to 7 minutes. Pour into a small bowl to stop the cooking, and cool slightly.

3. Transfer the garlic-oil mixture to a blender and add the cooked nettles, chives, lemon zest, red pepper flakes, and 1/2 cup of the hot water. Blend until very smooth and velvety. Add more water as needed to loosen. Season with salt and pepper to taste.

4. Transfer the pasta to a large (12-inch) skillet and add the nettle sauce, cheese, and butter. Add a little pasta water to loosen the sauce if needed. Heat thoroughly, tossing. Season with salt and pepper to taste and serve with more Parmesan on the side.

I like the simplicity of this pasta without any embellishments, but a handful of peas or peeled fava beans is a good addition. You can also finish the sauce with a splash of cream instead of butter.

You can use this nettle sauce in a variety of ways besides over pasta. Serve it hot or cold on seafood like grilled or poached salmon, shrimp, or halibut, adding a little lemon juice to the sauce at the last minute. Or experiment with basil, parsley, chervil, mint, tarragon, or even arugula to nudge this sauce one way or the other. Substitute kale or spinach for the nettles for a similar effect.

HOW TO PICK AND PREP STINGING NETTLES

Nettles should come with the warning "Beware!" since their stems are covered with tiny hairs that release stinging chemicals. Put on your rubber dishwashing gloves before you handle them and wear long pants when harvesting them. (If you do get stung, don't worry; the itching will stop in a moment.) I snip off only the top leaves as I harvest, leaving the stems. Wash and dunk the nettles in boiling salted water just long enough to wilt them, then drain and refresh them in a bowl of ice water. Drain again and squeeze out the excess moisture. You can use them right away or store in the fridge for a day or two.

VEG FORWARD

SERVES 6 TO 8

GRILLED PIZZETTES WITH WHIPPED RICOTTA, ROASTED RADISHES, AND HERBS

These pillowy little pizzas are topped with creamy whipped ricotta after grilling, which anchors juicy roasted radishes (or almost any other vegetable you can think of; see note below). They're drizzled with a green oil made from the radish tops, which adds a grassy note, and showered with tender spring herbs and lemon zest for more zip. The small size of each piece of dough makes these relatively easy to cook on a grill, especially a gas grill where it's easier to control the heat.

For the dough

3/4 teaspoon active dry yeast

3/4 cup/177 ml warm water

1/2 teaspoon sugar

1 tablespoon extra-virgin olive oil

1 3/4 cups/224 g all-purpose flour

3/4 teaspoon kosher salt

For the roasted radishes

1 bunch French breakfast radishes or other small radishes, with their greens

1/2 cup extra-virgin olive oil, plus more for the radishes

Kosher salt and freshly ground pepper

For the topping

1 cup/8 ounces ricotta, preferably fresh

Grated zest of 1 lemon

1 tablespoon lemon juice

A handful of fresh soft herbs, such as chervil, tarragon, chives, parsley

Flaky sea salt

Instructions

1. **To make the dough:** In a small bowl, dissolve the yeast in the water. Stir in sugar and olive oil. Combine flour and salt in the bowl of a stand mixer using the paddle. Mix briefly to combine, and slowly pour in the yeast mixture on medium-low speed until well-combined. Mix for about 5 minutes until smooth and stretchy. Scrape into an oiled bowl and turn to coat the dough with oil. Cover with plastic wrap and let rise at room temperature until doubled in size, 1 to 2 hours.

2. **To roast the radishes:** Heat the oven to 400°F. Trim the radishes, leaving about 1/2 inch of the stem attached, and reserve the greens. Halve the radishes lengthwise and toss with enough oil to coat, and lightly season with salt and pepper. Spread out on a baking sheet and roast, stirring once or twice, for 15 to 20 minutes, or until just starting to turn golden brown on the cut sides. Transfer to a plate. Wash and dry about 1 cup of the greens. Put them in a food processor with the olive oil and process until smooth. Season to taste and transfer to a small bowl. Rinse out the food processor.

3. **To make the ricotta topping:** Process the ricotta with the lemon zest and juice in the food processor until smooth. Refrigerate until ready to use.

4. When the dough is ready, heat one side of a gas grill to medium. If using a charcoal grill, make sure to leave a cool side of the grill. Thoroughly oil the grill grates.

5. Turn the dough onto a lightly oiled baking sheet and divide into 2 pieces. Using oiled hands, stretch the dough into rounds or ovals and lightly oil them. Cover with plastic wrap and let rest for 10 minutes. Stretch a little larger as you transfer the pieces of dough to the hot side of the grill; don't worry if the shapes get wonky.

6. Cover the grill and turn the pizzettes after 2 to 3 minutes. Cook for 2 to 3 minutes longer, until charred in places but not burnt. If not quite done, move to the cooler side or the upper rack of the grill, until cooked through, another 2 to 3 minutes.

7. Spread with the ricotta, top with the radishes, drizzle with the radish oil, sprinkle with the herbs and flaky salt, and serve immediately, cut into serving pieces.

RADISH REVELATIONS

It's time to think about radishes as more than an afterthought on a green salad. Treat them as a full-fledged vegetable in their own right. When they're roasted, much of their sharp flavor is softened, and they become juicy. Try throwing them into mixed roasted vegetables. And don't forget to use the greens. If you get your radishes (or turnips) fresh from a farm, the greens are likely to be extremely fresh and delicious. They might be very sandy (so wash them thoroughly) and also a bit prickly, but that will disappear when you cook them.

VEG FORWARD

SERVES 4

ROASTED ASPARAGUS WITH BASTED EGGS AND PARM

When the first stalks of asparagus appear around Mother's Day each year, I make this simplest of dishes, which highlights and enhances the coveted spears. The basted egg is the poached egg's easier and less well-known cousin. It's steamed in a small amount of water, along with some butter for flavor, so the underside remains soft.

Ingredients

1 bunch (about 1 pound) asparagus, tough ends snapped off

2 teaspoons olive oil

Kosher salt and freshly ground pepper

1 tablespoon unsalted butter

1/4 cup water

4 large eggs

1 ounce shaved Parmesan

1 tablespoon fresh snipped chives

Toasted sourdough slices

Instructions

1. Heat the oven to 500°F, or the highest setting, with a baking sheet on the upper middle rack.

2. On a plate or baking sheet, drizzle the asparagus with olive oil and add salt and pepper, using your hands to coat them well.

3. Put the asparagus on the hot baking sheet and roast for 12 to 14 minutes, turning or tossing once. Set aside while you cook the eggs.

4. Heat a large (12-inch) nonstick skillet over medium heat. Add the butter and water. Crack the eggs into the pan and turn the heat down to medium-low. Cook, covered, for 3 to 4 minutes, or until the yolk is done to your liking.

5. Divide asparagus among four plates, and top each one with an egg, some Parmesan, and some snipped chives. Serve immediately with sourdough toast.

The asparagus are also wonderful grilled. Heat a grill with a grill platter or grill wok to high, then grill on medium-high for 2 to 3 minutes on each side.

SPRING TOAST WITH FRESH RICOTTA, FAVAS, AND ASPARAGUS

This creamy, crunchy toast is substantial enough for a quick meal, especially for lunch. Topped with tender favas and a few slender asparagus, the whole is much more than just the sum of its parts. Favas are a seasonal treat, but because they need to be popped out of their pods and skinned, I like to use them sparingly where they can make an impact, so I don't have to do lots of prep work. These toasts are a delicious way to stretch them when you have only a handful or two.

Ingredients

3/4 pound fava beans in their pods

8 thick asparagus

1 tablespoon olive oil, plus more for drizzling

1 small shallot, thinly sliced into rings

Kosher salt and freshly ground pepper

1 tablespoon water

4 thick slices sourdough bread, toasted or grilled

1 cup ricotta, preferably fresh

A big handful of fresh soft herbs like tarragon, mint, basil, chives, or dill

Grated zest of 1 lemon

Flaky salt

Instructions

1. Prep the fava beans according to the instructions below. Set aside. Snap the tough bottoms from the asparagus and cut on the diagonal into 1/2-inch pieces.

2. Heat a medium pan over medium heat and add the olive oil. Add the shallot and cook for 2 minutes, until translucent. Add the asparagus and season with salt and pepper. Add the water, cover, and cook for 2 to 3 minutes, until the asparagus are bright green.

3. Add the favas and cook uncovered for 1 to 2 minutes. Transfer the mixture to a plate to cool slightly.

4. Spread each slice of toast with a quarter of the ricotta. Divide the vegetable mixture among the toasts and top with a shower of herbs and lemon zest. Sprinkle with flaky salt and a drizzle of olive oil.

You can use fresh or frozen peas (no need to thaw) instead of favas.

HOW TO PREP FAVA BEANS

Favas require a bit of labor to free them from their pods and thick skins. First, shell them and discard the pods. Bring a small pot of water to a boil and drop the favas in. Let cook for 1 minute. Drain and rinse with cool water. With a pair of small kitchen scissors or your fingernail, cut or tear a little hole in the tough skin on one end of the bean. Then gently squeeze and the bright green bean will pop out.

SERVES 4 TO 6

ZUCCHINI, LEEK, AND POTATO SOUP

Quick and oh-so-comfortingly thick, this is a soup for those early spring days when there's still a chill in the air. I love its pure vegetable flavor, but you can finish it with a little milk or cream if you like.

Ingredients

1 tablespoon olive oil, plus more for drizzling

4 large or 6 small stalks of green garlic, sliced, or 2 to 3 large garlic cloves, sliced

3 cups sliced leeks (2 to 3 leeks)

Salt and freshly ground pepper

2 ½ pounds zucchini (3 large or 6 small), quartered lengthwise and cut 1 inch thick

3 medium (about 12 ounces) Yukon Gold potatoes, peeled and cut into 2-inch chunks

3 cups chicken or vegetable stock (page 226), plus more as needed

1 small Parmesan rind

Handful of fresh basil, torn into pieces (optional)

2 to 4 ounces milk or cream, or more as needed (optional)

Grated or shaved Parmesan for serving

Instructions

1. Heat oil in a medium Dutch oven or soup pot over medium-low heat. Add garlic and leeks and season with salt and pepper. Cook until softened, about 8 minutes. Add zucchini and potatoes, increase heat to medium, cover, and cook for 25 to 30 minutes, stirring occasionally, until zucchini is very soft and some liquid has accumulated in the pot.

2. Add stock and the Parmesan rind and cook uncovered over low heat, stirring occasionally, until potatoes are very soft, 20 to 25 minutes. Add the basil and adjust seasonings. Remove about 2 cups of the soup and puree in a blender or using an immersion blender. Of course, you can just blend right in the pot using the immersion blender, but I like to remove it so I don't accidentally overblend the soup and lose the chunky texture.

3. Return the puree to the soup, add milk or cream (if using; it's perfectly fine without it too), and add more water or stock if needed to thin to desired consistency.

4. Serve hot with grated Parmesan and a drizzle of olive oil.

If you have some garlic scapes, or even ramps, use them instead of the green garlic.

For a simple dinner that really hits the spot, add some chicken or turkey meatballs and a generous amount of Parmesan.

Regular supermarket zucchini works great here. Just make sure they're smooth and firm.

VEG FORWARD

21

MAKES 8 TOASTS

GARLIC SCAPE TOAST

This is garlic bread with an edge. Use the best sourdough you can get. Curly green garlic scapes, which are available most of the summer at farmers' markets, do everything garlic does, but better. They're milder, so they don't require cooking to be digestible, and they have a grassy freshness.

For the garlic scape pesto

6 garlic scapes, cut into roughly 1-inch pieces (about 3/4 cup)

1 cup Italian parsley and/or basil leaves and soft stems, lightly packed

6 tablespoons olive oil

1/2 teaspoon kosher salt

For the toast

1 tablespoon butter, melted

Half a 1-pound loaf sourdough bread, sliced 1 inch thick (8 slices)

Instructions

1. **To make the pesto:** Combine the scapes, herbs, oil, and salt in a food processor. Pulse until nearly smooth.

2. **To make the toast:** Stir together the pesto and butter and set aside.

3. Grill or broil the bread on medium for 1 to 2 minutes per side, or until slightly charred. Brush each piece with the pesto butter mixture and return to the grill buttered side down for 30 seconds, or until bubbling. Serve immediately.

I make this pesto and freeze it in ice cube trays and then transfer the cubes to a zip-top bag to use as needed so I can keep those fresh spring flavors going all year long by swirling it into hot or cold soup, stirring it into a hot or cold pasta dish, or adding to roasted vegetables. The frozen pesto will keep for at least several months.

VEG FORWARD

THE GREAT SCAPE

Farmers trim the scapes so the garlic plant can channel its energy into bulbs, rather than flowers. The tasty scapes can be used in myriad ways. I grill them whole, as a vegetable, similar to asparagus. I cut them into small pieces and sauté in oil to start a dish, as you would with chopped garlic.

Because scapes are so curly, they can be a little tricky to cut. I trim off the top section with the tapered point right where it meets the stalk (though I leave them on if I'm grilling them whole), then cut the scapes into manageable lengths of about 4 to 5 inches. From there you can more easily chop them into smaller pieces.

SERVES 4 (IF YOU'RE LUCKY)

FRENCH VEGETABLE SALAD WITH PICKLED SHALLOT VINAIGRETTE

When I first traveled solo to Paris when I was in my twenties, Parisians didn't speak as much English as they do now and there was no Instagram or internet, so finding good meals could be a challenge. One day I ordered an *assiette de crudités*, a plate filled with bright little piles of grated raw vegetables, most memorably carrots and beets. Inspired by that French classic, this salad, featuring mounds of grated carrots and beets as well as thinly sliced sugar snaps, asparagus, radishes, and fennel, is fancy looking but utterly simple. You can dress each vegetable individually before assembling, or drizzle dressing over the whole thing and toss together.

Ingredients

2 large or 4 regular carrots

1 large beet (about 8 ounces)

6 to 8 ounces sugar snap peas, strings removed

4 large asparagus

1/2 large fennel bulb, trimmed, fronds reserved

2 to 3 radishes

1 head Belgian endive (white or red)

Handful of fresh mint leaves

Pickled Shallot Vinaigrette (page 225)

1/2 cup hazelnuts, toasted and skinned

Chopped tarragon or dill

Kosher salt and freshly ground pepper

Instructions

1. Keeping the vegetable piles separate as you work, grate the carrots on the large holes of a box grater or with the grating blade of a food processor. Grate the beets. Sliver the snap peas vertically. Shave the asparagus into thin ribbons with a vegetable peeler and slice the remaining parts of the asparagus as thinly as possible by hand.

2. Shave the fennel thinly on a mandoline, if you have one, or with a sharp knife. Do the same with the radishes. Separate the leaves of the endive, leaving them whole and trimming the bottom as you go, and arrange in a shallow serving bowl. Toss the grated carrots with the mint and some of the dressing.

3. Arrange all the vegetables except for the radishes in the bowl in separate piles, saving the beets for last. After washing your beet-stained hands, scatter the radishes on top, along with the hazelnuts if you're using them, and a scattering of herbs. Drizzle a generous amount of dressing over top, serving extra on the side. Sprinkle salt and pepper over the salad and toss after presenting. Leftovers are good for 2 days.

This is a flexible template; use what you have and what you like and what's in season. In addition to the vegetables listed here, try finely shredded cabbage, grated daikon, celeriac, or kohlrabi. Add almonds instead of hazelnuts (or leave them off), add feta or goat cheese, chickpeas, or poached or grilled chicken breast to make it a full meal.

SERVES 4

LITTLE GEM AND RADISH SALAD WITH BUTTERMILK-FETA DRESSING

For this wedge salad, which begs to be eaten with a knife and fork, you need a crunchy lettuce that can stand up to the creamy dressing. Little Gem, the petite romaine variety that is increasingly common in markets, is perfect, or substitute romaine hearts.

For the dressing

3 ounces creamy, mild feta

1/4 cup thick yogurt (like Greek or Skyr)

1/4 cup buttermilk

1 tablespoon mayonnaise

Grated zest of 1 lemon

1 tablespoon lemon juice

1/4 teaspoon kosher salt

Freshly ground pepper

1 small garlic clove

For the salad

4 heads Little Gem romaine

1 ounce creamy, mild feta

2 large or 4 small radishes

1/4 cup chopped dill

Olive oil, for drizzling

Flaky salt and freshly ground pepper

Instructions

1. **To make the dressing:** Crumble the feta into a small bowl and add the yogurt, buttermilk, mayonnaise, lemon zest, lemon juice, salt, and pepper. Use a fork to combine, lightly mashing the feta and leaving some texture. If you like raw garlic, use a Microplane to grate the garlic in; otherwise crush the garlic clove and add to the dressing to let it gently infuse (you can remove it later). Set aside.

2. **To make the salad:** Trim the root end of the lettuce but leave enough intact to hold the heads together. Wash well and spin dry. Place 2 lettuce halves on each of four plates (or arrange on a platter). Drape the lettuce with a generous amount of dressing and crumble the feta over top.

3. Slice the radishes paper thin, using a mandoline or a sharp knife, and scatter on top, along with the dill. Drizzle with olive oil and sprinkle with salt and pepper. Serve any extra dressing on the side.

SERVES 2 TO 4

SIMPLEST ASPARAGUS

My favorite way to cook asparagus is hot and fast: grilled or roasted. I love the bit of char they get on the outside, while remaining juicy and tender within. They have enough personality to be served with drinks at cocktail hour, perhaps with a little aioli for dipping. They're the ultimate finger food.

Ingredients

1 pound asparagus

Olive oil

Kosher salt and freshly ground pepper

Garlic powder

Lemon juice (optional)

Flaky salt

Instructions

1. **To prep the asparagus**: Snap the tough bottoms off the asparagus and peel the bottoms of the thicker stalks if you want. Toss with enough oil to coat (2 to 3 teaspoons) and sprinkle lightly with salt and pepper. Don't oversalt, because as the thinner stalks shrink during cooking, they can become too salty. I also like to sprinkle them with a little garlic powder—it adds a little more savory flavor.

2. **To grill the asparagus**: If you're using a gas grill, heat a grill platter (see page 29) on a grill set to high heat and spread out the asparagus on the grill platter. Turn down to medium-high and grill for 2 to 3 minutes, until lightly charred, and turn. Grill for another 2 to 3 minutes, until the asparagus is charred on the outside and starts to look juicy. Cooking times will vary depending on the thickness of the spears. If your bunch contains thin and thick spears, remove them as they are finished.

3. **To roast the asparagus**: Heat the oven to 500°F, or the highest setting, with a baking sheet set on the upper middle rack. Carefully remove the hot baking sheet from the oven and spread the asparagus on the pan. Roast the spears until tender and browned, 12 to 14 minutes, tossing halfway through cooking time.

4. Serve the grilled or roasted asparagus with a squeeze of lemon if you want and some flaky salt.

If you don't have a grill platter, carefully arrange the asparagus perpendicular to the grill grates so they don't fall through, or take a large piece of heavy-duty foil and poke plenty of holes in it. This will shield the asparagus from the harshest heat of the grill.

VEG FORWARD

SERVES 4

SUGAR SNAP, CABBAGE, AND RADISH SLAW WITH BUTTERMILK DRESSING

Crunchy, juicy raw sugar snaps, frilly napa cabbage, and crisp, sharp radishes tossed in an herby, creamy, and slightly spicy dressing make this slaw a craveable side dish for fish or chicken—or all on its own. The slaw keeps well, even improving after a day in the fridge.

For the dressing

1/2 small garlic clove, sliced

A few slices jalapeño to taste

1/4 cup thick Greek yogurt

1/4 cup buttermilk

2 tablespoons coarsely chopped herbs, such as tarragon, mint, and chives

1/2 tablespoon olive oil

1/4 teaspoon kosher salt

Freshly ground pepper

For the slaw

1/2 head (6 ounces/170 g) napa cabbage, thinly sliced

Salt and pepper

8 ounces sugar snap peas, strings removed and sliced lengthwise

1/3 cup/1 ounce watermelon radish (or any kind of radish), very thinly sliced on a mandoline or with a sharp knife

Instructions

1. **To make the dressing:** Combine the garlic, jalapeño, yogurt, buttermilk, herbs, olive oil, salt, and pepper in a mini food processor and blend until smooth.

2. **To make the slaw:** Toss the cabbage with the dressing and season with salt and pepper. Add the snap peas and radish and toss to combine. Adjust the seasonings if necessary and top with more herbs.

Sugar snap peas are especially good raw, but you can give them a 10-second dunk in some boiling water, followed by an ice bath if you prefer, which will brighten the color and soften the texture.

Keep your eyes peeled for purple napa cabbage; it adds gorgeous color.

SERVES 4 TO 6

COLCANNON WITH NETTLES

The traditional Irish dish of mashed potatoes with greens and leeks or scallions and lots of cream and butter makes a welcoming home for nettles. I look forward to foraging them each spring in my secret patch, and I always cook them as soon as I get them—not only so they'll be ready to use and save space in the fridge, but to take the sting out of them. Blanch them quickly in boiling salted water and then refresh in ice water. Squeeze all the water out of them and store in the refrigerator for a few days or freeze for a few months. A butter pool on top of the potatoes is de rigueur.

Ingredients

1 pound Yukon Gold potatoes, peeled and halved if large

1 pound russet (Idaho) potatoes, peeled and halved

3 to 4 large garlic cloves

1 tablespoon kosher salt, plus more for seasoning

4 tablespoons (1/2 stick) unsalted butter, cut up, plus more for serving

2 cups sliced leeks (about 1 1/2 leeks, depending on size)

1 cup cooked nettles, roughly chopped (see page 13)

Freshly ground pepper

1 cup whole milk

1/2 cup heavy cream

Instructions

1. Place the potatoes and garlic in a large saucepan and cover by several inches with cold water. Add the salt. Bring to a boil, lower the heat to medium, and cook at a brisk simmer until the potatoes are easily pierced with the tip of a paring knife, 25 to 30 minutes. Drain in a colander.

2. Return the saucepan to medium-low heat and add the butter and the leeks. Cook until softened, 6 to 8 minutes. Add the nettles and season with salt and pepper. Cook for 1 minute. Add the milk and cream and bring to a boil.

3. Remove from the heat and add the potatoes and garlic and mash with a potato masher, taking care to mash the garlic cloves and incorporate them, leaving some texture. Season to taste and transfer to a serving bowl. Make a divot with the back of a spoon on the top and add an additional pat of butter, letting it melt into a puddle.

You can use kale or cabbage instead of the nettles. Spinach works too.

VEG FORWARD

HOW TO PREP LEEKS

When I get a bunch of leeks, I wash all of them and store whatever I don't use in an airtight container. I like to keep them handy to throw into other dishes like pastas, soups, or egg dishes. They will keep well for 4 or 5 days.

Leeks are usually sandy, so it's important to clean them well before using them. Start by cutting the hairy roots off the bottom. Then cut the dark green tops off, angling your knife toward the top of the leek to preserve the paler layers underneath. Cut the leek in half lengthwise and cut into 1/4-inch semicircles. (This size works for most recipes.) Scoop them into a large bowl of cold water and swish them around energetically to loosen any sand and grit. Let them sit for a few minutes to allow the sand to settle and scoop the leeks out (I use my hand) into a sieve or colander to let them drain. The one thing you should *not* do is pour the whole thing into a colander, because you'll be depositing all that sand back onto the leeks.

SERVES 4 TO 6

KOHLRABI-APPLE SALAD WITH POPPY SEEDS

With kohlrabi, daikon, celery, and apple, this salad is all crunch. You'll find kohlrabi in the market in the spring, and again in the fall, and they can vary from the size of an egg to the size of a softball. If yours are on the larger side, cut the rounds in half after slicing them to make them easier to eat. Granny Smith apples have the right level of tartness to play well with the other ingredients here and also lend a welcome hint of sweetness. Granny Smith also brown much less than other apple varieties, and once tossed in the dressing, they won't turn color at all. The salad tastes best after about an hour of marinating and will keep for a couple of days, though it gets a bit watery.

For the dressing

1 ¼ cups labneh or thick Greek yogurt

2 tablespoons lemon juice

1 ½ tablespoons olive oil

¾ teaspoon kosher salt

Freshly ground pepper

For the salad

1 pound kohlrabi bulbs (about 6 small or 4 medium), peeled

8 ounces daikon (2 small or ½ large), peeled

1 Granny Smith apple, cored and quartered

2 celery stalks, plus leaves

2 teaspoons poppy seeds

½ cup chopped dill

Instructions

1. **To make the dressing:** In a small bowl, combine the labneh or yogurt, lemon juice, and olive oil. Whisk until smooth and add salt and pepper to taste.

2. **To make the salad:** Use a mandoline or a sharp knife to slice the kohlrabi, daikon, and apples ⅛ inch thick. Slice the celery as thinly as possible by hand on the diagonal. Toss everything with the dressing and transfer to a serving bowl. Sprinkle the poppy seeds and the dill over top and serve.

You can cut the kohlrabi into matchsticks instead of slicing it.

VEG FORWARD

HOW TO PREP AND COOK KOHLRABI

Looking a bit like little green (or purple) UFOs, kohlrabi has become famous as the most befuddling vegetable in the CSA box. Though it's not a root vegetable, you can use it as you would one of them: roast in the oven, add it to a vegetable soup, or slice it into batons, boil, and serve with butter. It has a watery crunch and slightly sweet flavor, which makes it a great candidate for eating raw.

Trim the multiple little stems off, using a paring knife, to make the surface as smooth as possible, then peel with a vegetable peeler. To slice on a mandoline, hold on to the root end (with your hands sheathed in cut-proof gloves) and start slicing at the pointy end and stop when it starts feeling tough; the root end can be hard and fibrous.

VEG FORWARD

HOW TO STRING A SNAP PEA

Sugar snap peas, unless they're tiny and new, need to have the tough strings removed. The easiest way to do this is to grab the stem end at the top of the pod and snap it back so it breaks off, and then pull down, bringing the strings with it. Depending on how large the peas are, you might see two strings or just one. If it doesn't come off, then it's tender enough to eat.

SERVES 4

KALE AND SNAP PEA SALAD WITH SUNFLOWER SEED DRESSING

If you haven't massaged kale before, you haven't lived. It truly is the secret to a great kale salad. Because the size of a head of kale can vary so much, always start with less dressing and add more as needed. This one, with its nutty, earthy flavors from toasted garlic and sunflower seeds, coats the leaves luxuriously, while the bright and crunchy sugar snap peas add a spring-y element.

For the dressing

4 tablespoons olive oil, divided

2 large garlic cloves, cut into thick slices

1/3 cup shelled sunflower seeds

Kosher salt

2 tablespoons lemon juice (from 1 small lemon)

Splash of balsamic vinegar

1 teaspoon maple syrup

1/2 teaspoon kosher salt

Freshly ground pepper

1 tablespoon water

For the salad

Kosher salt

8 ounces sugar snap peas, strings removed

1 pound lacinato kale, leaves stripped from stems

Large handful fresh mint leaves

Instructions

1. **To make the dressing:** Put 2 tablespoons of the olive oil and garlic in a small skillet on medium-low heat and toast the garlic until almost golden on both sides, 6 to 8 minutes. Add the sunflower seeds and continue cooking until about half the seeds have turned brown, 4 to 5 minutes. Scrape onto a plate to cool.

2. Scoop half of the toasted seeds into a small bowl and season with salt to taste. Reserve for the topping.

3. Put the remaining seeds, along with the garlic and the oil from the pan, in a food processor. Add lemon juice, vinegar, the remaining 2 tablespoons of oil, maple syrup, 1/2 teaspoon salt, pepper, and water and blend until smooth. Set aside in a small bowl.

4. **To make the salad:** Bring a medium saucepan of salted water to a boil; add the snap peas and cook for 10 to 15 seconds, just until bright green. Drain, rinse, and refresh in a bowl of ice water. Drain again when cool, and pat dry. Cut into lengthwise slivers.

5. Add enough of the dressing to the kale to moisten it, holding some back to avoid overdressing. Season with salt and pepper to taste, then massage the kale with your hands to coat it with the dressing and break down the kale a little. Add the snap peas and toss to combine. Add more dressing if needed, and season with more salt and pepper to taste. Sprinkle the mint leaves and reserved sunflower seeds over top and serve.

VEG FORWARD

39

SERVES 4

SUNCHOKE SALAD WITH RADICCHIO AND FRIED CAPERS

In early spring, you might come across the odd-looking tubers of sunchokes—also known as Jerusalem artichokes—at your farmers' market. They can be treated the same way you would potatoes, but they cook a bit faster, and they can also be eaten raw—they're crunchy like an apple. (They don't need to be peeled, which is good, because it would be difficult to do with all their little protrusions.) Here they're simply roasted and added to a plate of radicchio along with crunchy, fried capers and a wedge of cheese. This salad makes a very elegant lunch.

For the sunchokes

1 tablespoon olive oil

12 ounces sunchokes (8 to 10)

2 sprigs fresh thyme

Kosher salt and freshly ground pepper

For the capers

2 tablespoons vegetable oil

2 tablespoons large capers, rinsed and patted very dry

For the dressing

1 tablespoon red wine vinegar

1/2 teaspoon Big Batch Roasted Garlic (page 217) or 1 small garlic clove, grated

Kosher salt and freshly ground pepper

2 tablespoons extra-virgin olive oil

For the salad

4 cups torn radicchio, preferably a mild variety such as Grumolo Rosso or Castelfranco

4 ounces soft goat cheese

Instructions

1. **To roast the sunchokes:** Heat the oven to 425°F. Drizzle the oil on a baking sheet and toss the sunchokes and thyme in the oil, coating well. Season with salt and pepper and roast until browning on the first side (about 25 minutes). Carefully turn using an offset spatula or another spatula (if they're sticking, just let them rest out of the oven for a few minutes before turning, loosely covered with foil) and cook for 10 minutes more until golden on both sides.

2. **To fry the capers:** Meanwhile, heat the oil in a small skillet over medium heat. Add the capers and cook for 1 to 2 minutes until they've burst open and crisped up. Transfer to a paper towel to drain.

3. **To make the dressing:** Whisk the vinegar, garlic, salt, and pepper together in a small bowl. Slowly whisk in the oil.

4. **To assemble the salad:** Lightly dress the radicchio and season with salt and pepper. Arrange on plates and top with the sunchokes and fried capers. Serve a wedge of cheese on each salad.

You can use whatever greens you like: spicy arugula, bitter radicchio, or the slightly sweeter Belgian endive all work well.

Try making the salad with fingerling potatoes or any small potato instead of the sunchokes.

I love the way an ash-covered soft goat cheese looks and tastes here, but you can use any goat cheese or even a runny, bloomy rind brie-type cheese or a washed rind cheese like Taleggio.

VEG FORWARD

41

MAKES 4 (8-BY-5-INCH) TARTS, EACH SERVING 2 TO 4

RHUBARB GALETTES WITH HAZELNUT FRANGIPANE AND CANDIED HAZELNUTS

These mini galettes have it all: They're sweet, tart, salty, soft, crunchy, flaky, and buttery. The hazelnut filling provides a luxurious buttery base for the rhubarb, echoing the salted candied hazelnuts on top (see page 220). I like to line up the rhubarb strips horizontally on the pastry, but you can go free-form if you want. None of the components of this dessert are difficult, and they all add up to something special.

For the crust

2 cups/256 g all-purpose flour

3/4 teaspoon kosher salt

1 tablespoon granulated sugar

14 tablespoons/198 g (1 3/4 sticks) cold unsalted butter, cut into 1/2-inch slices

1/4 cup ice water, plus more if needed

For the frangipane

8 tablespoons/113 g (1 stick) unsalted butter, softened

1/2 cup/100 g granulated sugar

1/2 teaspoon kosher salt

1 cup/90 g hazelnut flour or 2/3 cup/90 g whole toasted and skinned hazelnuts, ground

1 large egg

1 teaspoon vanilla extract

For the rhubarb

1 vanilla bean, split lengthwise

1/4 cup granulated sugar

1 pound trimmed rhubarb stalks

2 tablespoons lemon juice (from 1 lemon)

2 tablespoons coarse sugar, like Sugar in the Raw

To finish

Salted Candied Hazelnuts (see page 220)

Instructions

1. **To make the crust:** Put the flour, salt, and sugar in a food processor and pulse until combined. Add the butter and pulse until the largest pieces are the size of walnut halves. Transfer to a wide bowl and squeeze the butter pieces, flattening them between your fingers. Sprinkle the ice water over the flour mixture and mix it in evenly, tossing with a fork. If there are a lot of loose, dry crumbs at the bottom of the bowl and the dough won't hold together when squeezed, add up to 2 tablespoons more ice water, 1 tablespoon at a time.

2. Press the dough together, gathering up any dry bits until the dough forms a shaggy, cohesive mass. Transfer to a sheet of plastic wrap. Wrap tightly and press into a flat rectangle. Shape the edges with your hands so they are not crumbly. Refrigerate until firm, at least 1 hour and preferably 2, and up to 2 days ahead (or freeze for up to 3 months).

3. **To make the frangipane:** Cream the butter, sugar, and salt in the bowl of a stand mixer or in a large bowl with a hand mixer. Add the hazelnut flour, egg, and vanilla and mix to combine.

4. **To prep the tarts:** Heat the oven to 400°F, with a rack in the middle. Line two baking sheets with parchment paper or silicone baking mats. Let the dough soften slightly at room temperature until malleable enough to roll out. Cut the dough into 4 equal pieces and on a lightly floured surface, roll one piece at a time (keeping the rest of the dough chilled) into a 7-by-10-inch rectangle, keeping the edges as uniform as possible. Place 2 rectangles side by side on each of two baking sheets. Use an offset spatula to spread the frangipane among the rolled-out pieces of dough, dividing it evenly, and leaving a 1-inch border. Refrigerate for at least 15 minutes until firm.

5. **To assemble the tarts:** Scrape the seeds from the vanilla bean and in a small bowl, rub the vanilla into the sugar until the flecks are evenly distributed. Cut the rhubarb into 4 1/2-inch lengths, then quarter them lengthwise. In a large bowl, toss the rhubarb with the lemon juice, then with the vanilla sugar.

6. Top each piece of dough with the rhubarb, lining the pieces up crosswise, and pour any leftover juices over the tops of the tarts. Fold the dough over to enclose just the edges of the filling, pressing down firmly so they don't open up in the oven. Chill again until firm, 15 to 30 minutes.

7. Brush the exposed pastry with cold water and sprinkle with coarse sugar. Bake for 30 to 40 minutes, until the juices are bubbling and the crust is deep golden brown.

8. Transfer to a cooling rack. Serve warm or at room temperature. Sprinkle with the candied hazelnuts just before serving.

SERVES 6

STRAWBERRY TARTLETS WITH GOAT CHEESE FILLING

When strawberries are at their peak, I serve them as simply as possible: over a creamy, tart filling in a delicate, crackly crust—polite but delicious supporting players. This is a kind of do-it-yourself tart kit whose components can be made ahead of time and carted off to your friend's house or a picnic for last-minute assembly. You can use any individual tartlet molds, but I especially like French flan rings. They are a little trickier to work with, since they have no bottom (they look like bracelets), but I like the modern lines and the large capacity of the shells as opposed to the fluted kind.

For the tart shells

1 1/2 cups/192 g all-purpose flour, plus more for rolling

1/3 cup/34 g confectioners' sugar

1/4 teaspoon kosher salt

1/4 teaspoon baking powder

8 tablespoons/113 g (1 stick) cold unsalted butter, cut into pieces

2 large egg yolks, lightly beaten

For the filling

4 ounces soft, mild goat cheese

1/4 cup plus 2 tablespoons/47 g confectioners' sugar

1/2 teaspoon pure vanilla extract or vanilla bean paste

8 ounces crème fraîche

For the strawberries

4 cups/1 pound strawberries, hulled and sliced in half, quartered if large

2 tablespoons granulated sugar

1 tablespoon Aperol (optional)

Instructions

1. **To make the tart shells:** Pulse the flour, confectioners' sugar, salt, and baking powder in a food processor. Add the butter and pulse to combine until it is in small pea-sized pieces. With the food processor running, slowly add the egg yolks through the feed tube. Stop the machine just as the dough begins to come together. Transfer the dough to a flour-dusted surface and knead it once or twice to make sure it is well mixed. Wrap the dough in plastic, flatten it into a disk, and refrigerate until firm, at least 1 hour.

2. **To make the filling:** In the bowl of a stand mixer with a paddle attachment (not a food processor), blend the goat cheese, confectioners' sugar, and vanilla at medium speed until smooth. Add the crème fraîche and gently mix at low speed until just combined. Transfer to a bowl and refrigerate until needed.

3. **To bake the tart shells:** Heat the oven to 375°F. Line a baking sheet with a silicone baking mat or parchment paper. Divide the dough into 4 pieces; refrigerate 3 of the pieces. On a well-floured surface, roll one piece of dough into a circle that is about 1/8 inch thick and slightly larger than the tart rings you are using. Press the dough into a tart ring, allowing the excess to hang over. Roll over the top of the tart ring with a rolling pin to remove the excess dough. Repeat with the other 3 pieces of dough, then reroll scraps as needed to fill all 6 rings. Prick the dough all over with a fork, transfer the lined tart rings to the prepared baking sheet using a spatula, and refrigerate for 15 minutes, or until firm.

4. Line each tart shell with a piece of buttered foil, fill with dry beans or pie weights, and bake for 15 to 17 minutes, or until golden at the edges. Remove the foil and continue to bake, uncovered, until evenly golden, 3 to 4 minutes. Cool completely. (You can make the tart shells up to 2 days ahead.)

5. **To make the strawberries:** Mix the strawberries, sugar, and Aperol (if using) together in a large bowl and set aside to macerate for at least 10 minutes, until the sugar is dissolved and the strawberries look juicy, tossing occasionally.

6. **To assemble the tarts:** Divide the cream and berries among the tart shells, starting with a layer of cream and finishing with the berries. Serve immediately.

VEG FORWARD

You can make this as one big tart: Lightly butter sides and bottom of a 10-inch removeable-bottom tart pan. Roll the dough to a 13-inch circle, ¹/8-inch thick. Follow instructions on page 45 for blind-baking crust. Blind bake for 15 minutes. Remove weights, then bake 8 minutes until evenly golden. Fill the shell with the cream filling and chill for 1 to 2 hours before filling with berries.

SUMMER

VEG FORWARD

SERVES 4

SUNGOLD SPAGHETTI CARBONARA

Authentic spaghetti carbonara is made with eggs and little cubes of pancetta, guanciale, or sometimes bacon. It's a last-minute cook's salvation, the kind of thing that can be put together at a moment's notice—a very simple dish that's all in the execution and the quality of the ingredients. Adding Sungolds, the golden-orange cherry tomatoes that have a lot more sweetness than the red ones, brings sunny color and bright acidity to the rich pasta dish. Black pepper is an important seasoning—the name *carbonara* is a reference to the abundant black pepper that looks like bits of carbon—so it should be visible when you present the dish.

Ingredients

2 large eggs, at room temperature

2 large egg yolks, at room temperature

1/2 cup/1 ounce finely grated Parmesan, plus more for serving

1/2 cup/1 ounce finely grated pecorino, plus more for serving

4 ounces guanciale (jowl bacon) or pancetta (cured Italian bacon), cubed

1 tablespoon kosher salt, plus more if needed

1 pound dried spaghetti

1 pint Sungold tomatoes, halved (about 2 cups)

Freshly ground pepper

Instructions

1. Whisk the eggs and yolks in a small bowl until just combined. Whisk in the cheeses. Set aside.

2. Place the guanciale or pancetta in a large (12-inch) skillet and set over medium heat. Cook, stirring frequently, until the cubes are crisp on the outside and much of the fat has rendered out, 10 to 12 minutes. Scoop out the meat and drain on paper towels, leaving the fat in the pan. Remove the pan from the heat.

3. Meanwhile, bring a large pot of water to a boil and add the salt. Cook the spaghetti until al dente. Before draining the pasta, reserve about 1 cup of the cooking water.

4. Drain the pasta and add to the pan with the reserved fat. Stir in the egg mixture quickly, tossing to coat the pasta evenly. Add the tomatoes, season with plenty of black pepper, and toss again. Add a little of the reserved pasta water (start with 1/4 cup) to thin out to the desired creamy consistency. Add salt to taste if needed. If the sauce needs thickening, heat the pan, gently tossing, until the sauce clings to the pasta. Add the reserved meat.

5. Divide among bowls, top each serving with a few grinds of pepper, and serve immediately, with more grated cheese on the side.

Guanciale, a cured meat made from the jowl of the pig, is traditional for carbonara, but it can be a little tricky to find. Pancetta is the next best thing, but regular smoked bacon works too. Buy the thickest cut you can find and cut into little cubes.

You can substitute regular cherry tomatoes for the Sungolds.

VEG FORWARD

VEG FORWARD

SERVES 4 TO 6

GREEK SLAB SANDWICH

The easiest way to do sandwiches for a crowd is to make a big one and cut it into squares. This sandwich, an homage to the Greek salad, one of the most unpretentious and delicious salads ever, is made with the focaccia on page 211. Despite being a pull-apart bread, it's cohesive enough to slice crosswise into two large pieces. This is the kind of sandwich that gets better as it sits, making it perfect for a picnic.

Ingredients

½ loaf Pull-Apart Focaccia (page 211)

¼ cup black olive paste or tapenade

4 large lettuce leaves

1 roasted red bell pepper, cut into 1-inch-wide strips, or ½ cup jarred roasted peppers

8 to 10 Slow-Roasted Tomatoes (page 216), skins removed

1 mini cucumber, peeled and sliced ¼ inch thick

3 ounces feta cheese, sliced or crumbled

¼ cup loosely packed chopped dill

½ teaspoon dried Greek oregano

Olive oil for drizzling (optional)

Instructions

1. Slice the focaccia loaf in half using a serrated knife, creating 2 square-ish pieces. Reserve one of the halves for eating or freezing (it freezes well). Slice one of the halves in half crosswise and open the halves on a work surface.

2. Spread the olive paste or tapenade evenly on both sides of the bread. Cover the bottom half of the focaccia with lettuce leaves, followed by the roasted pepper and then the tomatoes.

3. Arrange the cucumbers over the surface and crumble the feta over top. Sprinkle the dill and oregano over top, and finish with a drizzle of olive oil if desired. Close the sandwich and cover with a baking sheet weighted with a few heavy cans for 30 minutes. Cut into 4 to 6 pieces. If traveling to a picnic, wrap each piece with foil to hold it together.

You can use fresh tomatoes instead of slow-roasted; just keep in mind that they can turn the sandwich soggy, so try to serve soon after assembling for the best results.

Some other ideas for focaccia slab sandwiches (but feel free to let your imagination run wild—you know how to make a sandwich):

Sautéed greens (broccoli rabe, kale, mustard, Swiss chard) and ricotta

Shaved zucchini, tomatoes, goat cheese, pesto

Mashed avocado, grated carrots, Monterey Jack

Roasted or grilled vegetables with mozzarella (this one can be heated in the oven for a melty version)

HOW TO ROAST A PEPPER

Although you can buy roasted peppers in a jar, the ones you make yourself taste so much better, plus they create their own juicy sauce when freshly made. If you have a gas grill, you can throw them on anytime, but they can also be blackened directly on a gas-stove burner indoors or even under the broiler.

Heat a gas grill to medium-high. Place the peppers on the grill and cook, turning occasionally, until blackened all over, about 15 minutes.

Transfer to a plastic bag and set aside until cool. Use the bag to help you peel the peppers; most of the skin will slide right off. Leave behind all the skin and as many seeds as possible in the bag.

Cut out the stem and gently rinse just the inside of the pepper to wash away any remaining seeds, avoiding the outside where all that good, charred flavor is.

Store in an airtight container for several days.

SERVES 4 TO 6

FARRO AND SWEET RED PEPPER BAKE

This nutty, cheesy vegetable and grain bake is perfect for the end of summer when the weather turns cooler and peppers and tomatoes are abundant. Think of the farro as a stand-in for pasta. The concentrated flavor of slow-roasted tomatoes (page 216) gives the dish a special flavor, but sun-dried tomatoes stand in nicely.

Ingredients

2 small red bell peppers or 6 smaller thin-skinned red peppers like Jimmy Nardello (about 8 ounces), stemmed, seeded, and cut into 1/2-inch wide strips

2 medium red onions, sliced (1 1/2 cups)

1 1/2 tablespoons olive oil

Kosher salt and freshly ground pepper

4 cups cooked pearled farro (from 2 cups dry)

8 large Slow-Roasted Tomato halves (page 216), chopped (about 1 cup)

2 ounces thinly sliced soppressata, sliced into ribbons (optional)

1/2 teaspoon smoked paprika

1 tablespoon chopped fresh rosemary

1/2 cup water or vegetable stock (page 226)

3 ounces ricotta, preferably fresh

3 ounces fontina cheese, grated or cubed

Instructions

1. Heat the oven to 425°F. In a large (12-inch) cast-iron skillet, enameled cast-iron gratin, or ceramic or glass baking dish, coat the peppers and onions with the olive oil and season with salt and pepper. Roast for 25 to 30 minutes, stirring once or twice, until the onions are softened and the peppers are starting to brown. Remove from the oven and lower the heat to 400°F.

2. Stir in the farro, tomatoes, soppressata (if using), paprika, rosemary, water or stock, and salt and pepper to taste. Dollop the ricotta on top and sprinkle with the fontina.

3. Bake for 25 to 30 minutes, or until heated through and the cheese is melted and spotted with brown. Serve warm.

In place of the slow-roasted tomatoes, you can use sun-dried tomatoes soaked in water or jarred ones packed in oil.

Tomato water (page 227) can be used in place of water or stock.

HOW TO COOK PEARLED FARRO

Most of the farro you find at the store is pearled, meaning the bran and germ has been completely removed. Semi-pearled or whole farro will take longer to cook. Always rinse farro before using. Combine the farro and water at a ratio of 1:2 in a small saucepan. Add 1/4 teaspoon salt per cup of farro and a splash of your favorite vinegar if you want. Bring to a boil, reduce the heat to a simmer, cover, and cook on low heat for 15 to 20 minutes, until all the water has been absorbed.

Alternatively, you can cook the farro "pasta style": bring a large saucepan of water to a boil, add salt (and vinegar if desired), stir in the farro, and cook for 15 to 20 minutes until the grains are just beginning to split.

VEG FORWARD

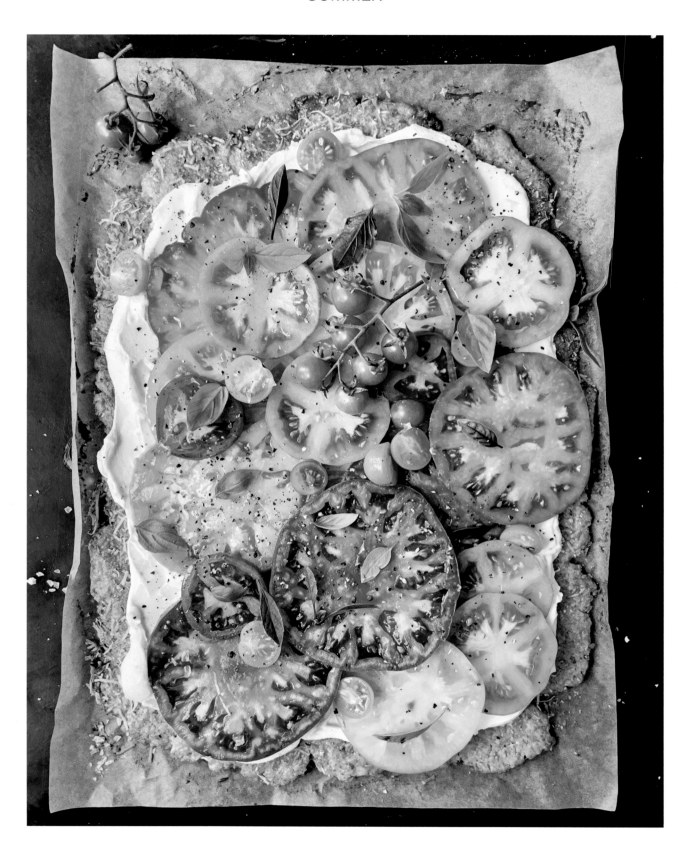

SERVES 4 AS A MAIN OR 6 TO 8 AS PART OF A SPREAD

HEIRLOOM TOMATO TART

Despite its stunning good looks, this tart is surprisingly easy to put together. It's much like a fresh fruit tart: just the crust is baked. A creamy ricotta–goat cheese filling is then spread over that, followed by the tomatoes, artfully arranged on top. The free-form crust, which is made a bit crumbly and tangy by some goat cheese standing in for some of the butter, stays crisp under the barrier of the creamy filling, preventing the tomato juices from invading. The tart can travel happily to a potluck or a picnic with little loss of quality. Leftovers will keep well in the fridge for a day or two.

For the dough

1 cup/128 g all-purpose flour, plus more for rolling dough

1 cup/120 g light rye flour

1 teaspoon granulated sugar

1/2 teaspoon kosher salt

1/8 teaspoon cayenne pepper

1 tablespoon fresh thyme leaves

8 tablespoons/113 g (1 stick) cold unsalted butter

3 ounces soft goat cheese

1/4 cup/59 ml ice water, plus more if needed

For the filling

7 ounces soft goat cheese

1/3 cup ricotta, preferably fresh

2 to 4 tablespoons whole milk

1 tablespoon extra-virgin olive oil

For the tart

1 large egg yolk

1 tablespoon heavy cream

1/2 ounce Parmesan cheese, finely grated (2 1/2 tablespoons)

3 to 4 assorted heirloom tomatoes (about 2 pounds)

Flaky sea salt and freshly ground pepper

Extra-virgin olive oil for drizzling

Fresh basil leaves, left whole if small, otherwise shredded

Instructions

1. **To make the dough:** Combine both flours, sugar, salt, pepper, and thyme in a food processor. Pulse to combine. Cut the butter into tablespoon-size pieces and toss into the bowl, along with the goat cheese. Pulse until the butter is broken down into almond-to-pea-size pieces. Transfer to a wide bowl and continue to break down the butter by combing your hands through the flour mixture and flattening the butter chunks between your fingertips (but work quickly to keep the butter cold).

2. When there are no more large chunks of butter left, drizzle in the ice water while using a fork to toss and stir. If the dough is too dry and crumbly, dribble in a tiny bit more water. Knead once or twice, then form into a rough rectangle and wrap in plastic wrap. Press down and use a bench scraper or your hands to form it into an even better rectangle, 1 to 1 1/2 inches thick. Refrigerate for at least 1 hour and up to 2 days or freeze for up to a month. When ready to use, soften the dough for about 30 minutes before attempting to roll it out.

3. Heat the oven to 400°F, with a rack in the middle of the oven. Roll out the dough on a lightly floured 12-by-16-inch piece of parchment paper, taking care to retain the roughly rectangular shape. Roll from the center out, flouring as needed until you have an 11 1/2-by-15-inch rough rectangle. Pick up the parchment by opposite corners and transfer to a baking sheet. Pop it back into the refrigerator to chill while you make the cheese filling.

4. **To make the filling:** Combine the goat cheese, ricotta, 2 tablespoons of the milk, and the olive oil in a food processor and process until smooth. Add more milk by the tablespoonful if needed until it has the consistency of smooth, thick cake frosting.

5. **To bake and assemble the tart:** Prick the dough all over with a fork. In a small bowl, combine the egg yolk and heavy cream, beating with a fork. Brush the entire surface of the dough with the egg wash and sprinkle evenly with the Parmesan. Bake for 15 to 20 minutes, or until deep golden brown all the way to the center. Cool completely on the baking sheet.

6. Using an offset spatula or the back of a spoon, spread the cheese mixture all over the crust, leaving a narrow border. Slice the tomatoes and layer them randomly on top of the cheese. Season with salt and pepper, drizzle with olive oil, and sprinkle with basil. Serve at room temperature.

VEG FORWARD

SERVES 6

ARBORIO-STUFFED TOMATOES WITH OLIVES AND HERBS

When I was a young cook, I was inspired by the food of Provence, and I had a classic book to take me there: *The Cuisine of the Sun* by Mireille Johnston. Back then you had to use your imagination when reading a cookbook, because there were no pictures (imagine that!). But I had no trouble dreaming up a magical life in Provence, where I'd be taking full advantage of the produce that hung heavily from garden vines.

Stuffed tomatoes, as I learned from the book, are a thing in Provence. The stuffing of these is extra creamy thanks to Arborio rice, which is cooked in the juice from the innards of the ripe tomatoes and punctuated with garlic, fresh herbs, and buttery oil-cured black olives. Prepping the tomato shells is the most time-consuming part of the recipe, but it's not difficult. The tomatoes can be made ahead of time and reheated when ready to serve.

Ingredients

6 medium (baseball-size) beefsteak tomatoes, ripe but firm

1 1/2 tablespoons olive oil, plus more as needed

1 small onion, minced

3 garlic cloves, minced

1 teaspoon fresh thyme leaves, chopped, or 1/2 teaspoon dried thyme

1 tablespoon tomato paste

1 cup Arborio rice

1/2 cup dry white wine

3/4 teaspoon kosher salt, plus more to taste

Freshly ground pepper

6 large basil leaves, cut into strips

1/2 teaspoon Calabrian chili paste, or 2 Calabrian chilies, minced, or big pinch of red pepper flakes (optional)

1/4 cup pitted oil-cured black olives, chopped

1 cup small cherry tomatoes (optional)

1 ounce Taleggio or fontina cheese (optional), cut into small pieces

Instructions

1. Heat the oven to 375°F, with a rack in the middle. Cut a thin slice off the top of each tomato and reserve. Cut along the wall of each tomato, leaving a 1/4 inch thickness around the side. Using a melon baller, a spoon, or your fingers, hollow out the inside of the tomato into the jar of a blender or food processor. If necessary, cut a very thin slice off the bottom of the tomato so it sits flat. Set the hollowed tomatoes aside. Puree the tomato pulp until smooth and push through a sieve to strain out the seeds.

2. Heat a large (12-inch) skillet or wide, shallow saucepan over medium heat. Add the oil and sauté the onion until softened, 5 to 6 minutes. Add the garlic and thyme and cook for 3 to 4 minutes.

3. Add the tomato paste and cook for 2 minutes, stirring constantly. Add the rice and a drizzle of oil and cook, stirring, for 2 minutes more. Add the wine and cook, stirring, until evaporated, about 1 minute.

4. Measure the tomato pulp; you'll need 3 cups. Add water if you have less than that. Add the liquid to the rice, along with salt and pepper to taste, bring to a boil, and reduce to a steady simmer. Cook for about 20 minutes, until the rice is still slightly al dente and just thick enough to mound a bit (it should not be completely soupy). Stir in the basil, Calabrian chilies or red pepper flakes, and the olives. Adjust the seasonings.

5. Arrange the tomatoes in a baking dish and spoon the rice mixture into them, dividing it evenly. Add 1/4 cup water to the baking dish. At this point, you can top the tomatoes with the reserved lids or add some whole or halved cherry tomatoes to the top and drizzle with a little oil. Bake for 40 to 45 minutes, until the tomatoes start to slump and the edges look juicy. If using the Taleggio or fontina, remove the pan from the oven in the last 5 minutes and dot the tops of the tomatoes with the cheese. Return to the oven to finish baking. Serve hot or at room temperature. You can cover and refrigerate the baked stuffed tomatoes for up to 1 day. To reheat, place the tomatoes in a baking pan and drizzle a tablespoon or two of water around them. Cover with foil and bake in a preheated 350°F oven for 15 to 20 minutes. Uncover and bake for 10 minutes longer, until heated through.

SUMMER

SERVES 4

SPOONBREAD-STUFFED POBLANOS WITH TOMATO CREAM

Fluffy, cakey corn pudding laced with scallions and Pepper Jack cheese is stuffed into whole roasted poblano chilies. A bit of cream and tart cherry tomatoes create an instant sauce right in the pan. Poblanos can be hot—or not. Either way, the packed-with-corn-flavor pudding will balance out the heat. Serve with a salad on the side.

Ingredients

4 large poblano peppers (about 1 pound)

1 cup whole milk

1 tablespoon butter

Kosher salt and freshly ground pepper

A big pinch of cayenne pepper

1/3 cup stone-ground cornmeal (preferably Bob's Red Mill medium grind)

1 cup corn kernels (from 1 large ear)

1 cup grated Pepper Jack cheese

4 large scallions, thinly sliced (about 1/2 cup)

1/2 teaspoon baking powder

2 large eggs, separated

1/2 cup heavy cream

1/2 cup (about 3 ounces) cherry tomatoes, preferably Sungolds

Instructions

1. To roast the poblanos, place the peppers directly over a gas flame on the stove, using one burner for 2 peppers at a time. Cook, turning every 2 or 3 minutes until charred all over, 6 to 8 minutes total. Transfer to a plastic bag to steam and cool, about 15 minutes.

2. Squeeze the peppers gently through the bag to remove most of the skin. Remove from the bag and peel any remaining skin. If the peppers naturally split, open them along this line. If not, cut a slit with a paring knife from the stem to the tip, keeping the stem intact. Gently rinse all the seeds from inside the pepper and blot dry with a paper towel. The peppers can be prepped to this point up to 2 days ahead.

3. Heat the oven to 400°F. Pour the milk into a small saucepan and add the butter, 3/4 teaspoon salt, a few grinds of pepper, and the cayenne. Whisk in the cornmeal and bring to a boil. Reduce the heat to medium-low and cook for 1 to 2 minutes, until thickened. Transfer to a bowl, stirring to speed cooling.

4. Add the corn kernels, cheese, scallions, and baking powder and stir to combine thoroughly. Stir in the egg yolks and blend well. In a separate, clean bowl, beat the egg whites with a pinch of salt until creamy and fluffy, but not dry. Stir half the egg whites into the corn mixture to lighten it, then fold in the remainder.

5. Arrange the peppers in a large baking dish with the slits facing up. Spoon the corn mixture into the peppers, dividing it evenly. Fold the peppers up somewhat to enclose the filling. Don't worry if it's not perfect. Season the cream with 1/4 teaspoon salt and pour it all around the peppers in the dish. Scatter the tomatoes around the peppers and bake for 35 to 40 minutes, until the cream is bubbling and the spoonbread is golden brown. Serve warm.

To roast the peppers under the broiler, line a small baking sheet with foil and line up the peppers on it. Set the pan about 6 inches away from the broiler and broil for 5 to 6 minutes per side, until the skin is charred. Steam, peel, and seed the peppers as directed.

To roast the peppers on a gas grill, set them over medium-high heat and cook for 10 to 15 minutes, turning to cook all sides until charred, 10 to 15 minutes.

VEG FORWARD

61

SERVES 4 AS A MAIN AND 6 TO 8 AS AN APPETIZER

SHEET-PAN ROASTED RATATOUILLE WITH SOCCA

Ratatouille is conclusive proof that what grows together goes together. In the classic version, each vegetable is cooked separately and then they are stewed together until creamy and homogeneous. My take is decidedly fresher and faster. The vegetables are roasted briefly on a sheet pan so they retain their individual characters. They're served on the crisp Provençal chickpea pancake, *socca*, creating a delightful pizza-like (but gluten-free) dish that can be served as a main course or in smaller pieces to go with an aperitif or chilled rosé.

Ingredients

1 small Japanese eggplant (4 ounces), cut 1/2 inch thick on the diagonal

2 small or 1 medium zucchini (10 ounces), cut into 1/2-inch-thick rounds

2 small or 1 large sweet red peppers (any kind), cut into strips

1 small red onion, cut into 1/4-inch-thick rings

Half a 15.5-ounce can chickpeas, drained, rinsed, and blotted dry

1 garlic clove, thinly sliced

2 tablespoons olive oil, plus 2 teaspoons more for the tomatoes

1/2 teaspoon kosher salt

Freshly ground pepper

1/2 pint cherry tomatoes (any kind, or a mix), halved

2 thick socca (Chickpea Pancakes; page 212)

4 ounces soft goat cheese

Flaky sea salt

8 to 10 basil leaves, shredded

Extra-virgin olive oil for drizzling (optional)

Instructions

1. Heat the oven to 425°F, with a rack in the middle. Toss the eggplant, zucchini, peppers, onion, chickpeas, and garlic with the 2 tablespoons olive oil, salt, and pepper on a large baking sheet. Make sure all the vegetables are well coated. Coat the cherry tomatoes with the remaining 2 teaspoons oil and set aside.

2. Roast the vegetables on the baking sheet for 25 minutes. Remove from the oven, stir and turn the vegetables, and scatter the tomatoes on the baking sheet. Cook for 10 to 15 minutes longer, until the vegetables have browned a little and the tomatoes are shriveled but still intact.

3. Warm the socca in the hot oven for 5 minutes in the skillet you cooked them in or on a small baking sheet and transfer to a serving plate. Crumble the goat cheese evenly over the socca and top with the warm vegetables. Sprinkle with flaky sea salt and basil. Add a drizzle of extra-virgin olive oil, if desired. Cut into wedges and serve warm.

I like Japanese eggplant for this recipe, because they're devoid of seeds, hold their shape, and are small enough to be cut into rounds, but any small eggplant can be used; just cut into bite-size pieces.

The same goes for zucchini. Baby zucchini (4 to 5 ounces each) work great and look nice cut into rounds, but if using larger zukes, quarter them lengthwise before cutting them 1/2 inch thick.

VEG FORWARD

63

MAKES 8 BLINTZES; SERVES 4 AS A MEAL

CHEESE BLINTZES WITH SOUR CHERRY COMPOTE

Blintzes are traditional for the Jewish holiday of Shavuot, but they are perfect anytime—for breakfast, brunch, lunch, or even dinner. The word *blintz* refers to the pancake itself, which is like a sturdy French crepe, but slightly thicker and more eggy. The cheese filling has a lemony tang. For the compote that's served over top, sour cherries are delicious. (They're in season for about a minute in the Northeast.) Unlike sweet cherries, which are larger and fleshier, sour cherries are tart and juicy. Every year, I pit and freeze as many as I have time to do, freezing them in a single layer on a sheet pan, and storing them in zip-top bags to use later. If you can't get them, berries are the next best choice (see notes on page 66).

For the pancakes

3 large eggs

1 cup/128 g all-purpose flour

1/4 teaspoon kosher salt

1 tablespoon granulated sugar

3/4 cup whole milk

1/4 cup cold water

Butter for cooking the blintzes

For the cherry compote

1 tablespoon cornstarch

3 tablespoons cold water

2 cups fresh or frozen pitted sour cherries

3 tablespoons granulated sugar

1 tablespoon lemon juice

For the filling

2 cups ricotta, preferably fresh

1/2 cup whipped cream cheese

1 large egg yolk

2 tablespoons granulated sugar

Zest of 1 lemon

1 tablespoon lemon juice

Butter for browning the blintzes

Confectioners' sugar (optional)

Instructions

1. **To make the blintzes:** Whisk together eggs, flour, salt, and sugar in a medium bowl until smooth. Combine milk and water and slowly whisk in until smooth (or you can do this in a blender). The batter can sit in the refrigerator for up to 1 day.

2. Slowly heat a medium nonstick skillet or crepe pan over medium heat. Add a small knob (about 1/2 teaspoon) of butter and swirl it around to coat the pan. Add a ladleful (about 1/4 cup) of batter to the pan, tilting the pan to coat completely. If you add too much batter, tilt the excess batter back into the bowl. You want just enough to coat the pan and not more.

3. Cook for 1 to 2 minutes on the first side, until the blintz looks dry in the center and is browning around the edges. Carefully flip and cook on the other side for about 1 minute. If the blintz seems fragile, cook it a little longer.

4. Slide the blintz onto a dinner plate. Repeat the process, adding a bit of butter to the pan each time until all the batter is used, stacking the blintzes directly on top of one another. At this point the blintzes can be wrapped and refrigerated for a day or two. Let the blintzes warm up at room temperature for a bit or for 20 seconds in the microwave to help them separate more easily.

5. **To make the compote:** Combine the cornstarch with water in a small dish. Stir together the cornstarch mixture, cherries, sugar, and lemon juice in a small saucepan. Bring to a simmer, stirring occasionally, until the cherries release their juices and the mixture thickens, about 5 minutes. Keep warm.

6. **To make the filling:** Combine the ricotta, cream cheese, egg yolk, sugar, lemon zest, and lemon juice in a small bowl. Mix thoroughly with a spoon.

7. Lay a blintz on a work surface with the browner side up. Spoon 2 to 3 tablespoons of the filling in the center and roll up like a burrito, folding the lower half of the pancake over the filling, folding in the sides, and rolling up to enclose the filling in a neat package. If you don't want to cook the blintzes right away, store them on a plate seam side down in the refrigerator for up to 1 day.

8. Melt 1 teaspoon butter in a large skillet over medium heat and add 4 blintzes to the pan, seam side down. Cook for 2 to 3 minutes on each side until golden brown. Wipe out the pan, add another teaspoon butter, and repeat.

9. Serve with some of the cherry compote spooned over top and dust with confectioners' sugar, if desired.

VEG FORWARD

You can sometimes find sour cherries frozen in health food stores, but if you can't get them, the blintzes are just as wonderful with blueberries or strawberries. Use the same quantity.

The ricotta cheese should look fairly dry. If it's at all runny, drain it in a paper towel–lined sieve for a few hours in the fridge to remove extra moisture.

The crepes cook best with just a small amount of butter—just enough to barely film the bottom of the pan. You will probably find they cook faster as the pan heats up, so adjust the heat accordingly, and watch them carefully.

SERVES 4 AS AN APPETIZER

ROASTED AND MARINATED SWEET RED PEPPER TOASTS WITH TOASTED GARLIC

Any sweet red pepper works here, but I particularly like the heirloom variety Jimmy Nardello for their thin skin and thinner-than-a bell-pepper wall of flesh, not to mention their sweet and fruity flavor. They have just a few seeds near the stem, so they're easy to prep too. The toasted garlic slices add a crunchy, savory element. The marinated peppers, which get more flavorful as they sit in the garlic-infused oil, are especially good piled onto crunchy pieces of toast spread with creamy cheese.

Ingredients

8 ounces sweet red peppers, preferably Jimmy Nardello

2 tablespoons olive oil, divided

4 large garlic cloves, sliced lengthwise

Handful of basil leaves

1/2 teaspoon kosher salt

Extra-virgin olive oil

4 ounces soft fresh cheese, like a good-quality creamy feta, goat cheese, or fresh ricotta

4 slices sourdough or ciabatta, toasted or grilled

Instructions

1. Split the peppers lengthwise and remove the stems and seeds. Coat them lightly with 1 tablespoon of the olive oil. Grill over medium-high for 2 to 3 minutes on the first side, and 1 to 2 minutes on the second side, or until softened and lightly marked by the grill.

2. Heat a small skillet over medium-low heat and add the remaining 1 tablespoon olive oil and the garlic. Cook, stirring, until golden, about 5 minutes.

3. Pour the garlic and oil over the peppers. Add the basil, salt, and extra-virgin olive oil. Toss to combine everything. The peppers can be used right away or marinated for up to 4 or 5 days.

4. Spread each piece of toast with some of the cheese and top with some of the peppers and the toasted garlic and serve.

These toasts are fabulous with Meredith Dairy cheese, which comes in a jar marinated in oil.

Tuck in a slice of soppressata if you want to make these more substantial.

VEG FORWARD

VEG FORWARD

SERVES 4 TO 6 AS AN APPETIZER

GRILLED CHERRY TOMATOES WITH YOGURT AND MINT

This recipe is way too easy to be this good. A few simple elements—yogurt, garlic, and grilled cherry tomatoes—come together quickly. A sprinkling of sumac adds a citrusy flavor and pretty burgundy color, but it's totally optional. What isn't optional is digging in with your friends, scooping it all up with warm flatbreads.

Ingredients

2 pints cherry or grape tomatoes

1 tablespoon extra-virgin olive oil, plus more for drizzling

1 cup thick Greek yogurt or labneh

1 small garlic clove, finely grated (optional)

Sumac, for sprinkling (optional)

Flaky salt and freshly ground pepper

Handful of mint leaves

Pita or flatbread for serving

Instructions

1. Heat the grill to medium-high. Toss the tomatoes with olive oil, place in a grill basket or wok, and cook for 4 to 5 minutes, until they are beginning to char. Shake the basket and cook for 3 to 4 minutes longer, until they begin to split and soften.

2. Mix the yogurt with the garlic (if using) and spread on a serving platter. Tumble the tomatoes on top. Sprinkle with sumac (if using), salt and pepper, and fresh mint leaves. Drizzle with the olive oil and serve with warm pita or flatbread.

VEG FORWARD

73

SERVES 4 TO 6

TOMATO WATER LEMONADE

The tomato flavor in this lemonade is subtle, but is even more refreshing than plain lemonade. Spike it with gin (my choice) or vodka for a quaffable cocktail.

Ingredients

1 1/2 cups Tomato Water (page 227)

1/2 cup lemon juice

2 cups water

2 tablespoons superfine or granulated sugar

Mint sprigs

Lemon slices

Instructions

1. Combine the tomato water, lemon juice, water, and sugar in a pitcher, stir to dissolve the sugar, and refrigerate until ready to serve.

2. Add some mint sprigs to the bottom of four to six serving glasses and use a wooden muddler or the handle of a wooden spoon to bruise the mint. Fill the glasses with ice and pour the lemonade over. Garnish with lemon slices and serve.

VEG FORWARD

SUMMER

ZUCCHINI AND SQUASH BLOSSOM QUESADILLAS

I like to imagine I'm in Oaxaca when I make these simple quesadillas. If you are lucky enough to find (or grow) squash blossoms, you know they have to be used quickly, before they spoil. These can be made on a moment's notice as long as you have the ingredients on hand. If you have a batch of Salsa Macha (page 214) in the fridge, it's the perfect condiment here. Drizzle it on before sandwiching the filling.

Ingredients

4 ounces fresh mozzarella, Oaxaca cheese, or string cheese

4 (7-inch) flour tortillas

1 small zucchini, shaved lengthwise with a vegetable peeler

Kosher salt

2 zucchini blossoms, petals removed from stamens

A few sprigs of cilantro

Instructions

1. Divide the cheese between 2 of the tortillas, then top with zucchini and season with salt to taste. Add the zucchini blossoms and cilantro, then top with the remaining tortillas.

2. Heat a skillet over medium-high. Place a quesadilla in the skillet and cook for 1 to 3 minutes per side, until the tortilla is brown and crisp and the cheese is melted. Repeat with the second quesadilla and serve immediately.

VEG FORWARD

SERVES 4 TO 6

COLD CUCUMBER AND AVOCADO SOUP

There's nothing better on a sweltering day than a bowl of cold soup. This one is as simple as a smoothie to make. The typical cold cucumber soup gets a rich upgrade from the creamy avocado, and some spicy kick from arugula. A fresh garnish of sugar snap peas adds crunch and textural variety.

Ingredients

3 medium cucumbers (1 1/4 pounds), peeled, seeded if necessary, and cut into chunks

1 Haas avocado, pitted and quartered

2 cups arugula

1 cup loosely packed soft herbs, such as mint, basil, chives, or chervil, plus more for garnish

1 garlic clove

1/4 cup lime juice (from 2 limes)

1 tablespoon rice vinegar

2 tablespoons extra-virgin olive oil, plus more for drizzling

Green sriracha or your favorite hot sauce to taste

1 cup plain Greek yogurt, plus more for serving

1 1/2 cups buttermilk

1 teaspoon kosher salt, plus more to taste

Freshly ground pepper

1 cup sugar snap peas, thinly sliced lengthwise

Instructions

1. Add the cucumbers, avocado, arugula, herbs, garlic, lime juice, rice vinegar, 2 tablespoons of olive oil, hot sauce, yogurt, buttermilk, salt, and pepper to taste to a blender and blend until smooth. Refrigerate before serving.

2. Top with a dollop of yogurt, herbs, the snap peas, a drizzle of olive oil, salt and pepper to taste, and serve.

If sugar snap peas aren't around when you make this soup, just cut up an extra cucumber for the garnish.

VEG FORWARD

79

SERVES 4 AS AN APPETIZER

ZUCCHINI TOASTS WITH FONTINA AND TALEGGIO

This recipe works especially well with small, dense zucchini that come early in the season. They're not as watery as large ones and have no seeds, and therefore they have more flavor. If you can't find small zucchini, just use the smallest you can find. Fontina and Taleggio are both great melting cheeses, with Taleggio adding a little funk.

Ingredients

2 small or 1 large zucchini (8 ounces), halved lengthwise if medium (or quartered if large) and sliced about 1/2 inch thick

1/4 teaspoon kosher salt

Freshly ground pepper

2 (3/4-inch-thick) slices sourdough, halved (4 pieces total)

3 ounces fontina, thinly sliced

1 ounce Taleggio, sliced (optional)

Basil, thinly sliced

Smoked chili flakes or red pepper flakes for topping

Fennel fronds, for garnish (optional)

Instructions

1. Heat the oil in a medium skillet over medium-high heat. Add the zucchini, salt, and pepper. Cook for 5 minutes, turning occasionally, or until golden brown. Remove from the heat and set aside.

2. Toast the bread under the broiler for 1 to 2 minutes per side, or in a toaster. Pile the fontina onto the bread, followed by zucchini. Broil on the center rack until the cheese is melted. Remove from the oven, dot the tops with Taleggio, and return to the broiler for another 1 1/2 minutes, or until melted. Top with the basil and pepper flakes and serve immediately. Garnish with fennel fronds (if using).

You can add a little pecorino or Parmesan for more complexity if you want.

SERVES 6

SIMPLE GAZPACHO

As soon as tomato season starts, it's gazpacho season at our house. Traditionally, gazpacho is thickened with bread and has copious amounts of olive oil, which helps to emulsify it and make it creamier. I prefer this fresher-tasting, almost calorie-free version. I often have a lot of tomato scraps around from slicing tomatoes for salads, and after trimming out any cores, I throw them in a container in the fridge, along with a splash of vinegar and some sliced garlic, which mellows as it sits in the acidic juice. When I have critical mass, I make this soup, usually adding some more fresh tomatoes. The amounts here are flexible—a little more of this or less of that won't make a big difference. Just adjust the seasonings, including more vinegar if needed after it's had a chance to chill.

Ingredients

6 medium or 4 large tomatoes (about 2 pounds), cut into chunks, and/or tomato scraps (about 6 cups)

2 large garlic cloves, sliced

2 tablespoons sherry vinegar, plus more to taste

1 teaspoon kosher salt

Freshly ground pepper

1 to 2 tablespoons extra-virgin olive oil

1 small or half large sweet onion (8 ounces), thinly sliced

1 large (14 ounce) cucumber, cut into chunks (about 2 cups)

2 red bell peppers

For the garnish

1 red or yellow bell pepper, cut into ¼-inch chunks

1 large cucumber, cut into ¼-inch chunks (about 2 cups)

1 cup/6 ounces cherry tomatoes, sliced in half

Finely diced jalapeño, to taste

Hot sauce

Instructions

1. In a large bowl, combine the tomatoes with the garlic, vinegar, salt, pepper, oil, onion, cucumber, and bell pepper and marinate for at least 1 hour.

2. Blend half the marinated vegetables in a high-speed blender until smooth and pour into a large bowl. Repeat with remaining vegetables. Transfer to a large container that will fit in your fridge.

3. Stir in the chopped vegetables and the hot sauce to taste. Refrigerate for a few hours. Adjust seasonings with salt, pepper, and vinegar to taste, and serve. It will keep well for 4 or 5 days.

Add diced ripe avocado.

Float olive oil–toasted croutons on top.

Add cooked shrimp, lobster, or crabmeat.

Add fresh herbs.

Add a drizzle or more of good olive oil.

VEG FORWARD

83

SERVES 4 AS A FIRST COURSE

WATERMELON, CUCUMBER, AND TOMATO WATER SALAD

This unbelievably refreshing and light soup-salad hybrid makes a very nice plated first course for a warm summer day or evening. The "broth," which is as clear as water but tastes intensely of the essence of tomatoes, is made from tomato water, which is a good use for all the tomato scraps that you might end up with this time of year. A small scoop of tart lemon sorbet floated on top wouldn't be wrong.

For the broth

2 cups Tomato Water (page 227)

½ teaspoon kosher salt, plus more to taste

1 tablespoon extra-virgin olive oil

For the salad

¼ medium seedless watermelon, rind cut off (about 1 ½ pounds), chilled

2 mini cucumbers, peeled

Assorted tomatoes (1 to 2 heirlooms, handful of cherry tomatoes)

Small handful shiso or basil, cut into thin strips

Small handful fresh mint, cut into thin strips

1 small jalapeño, very thinly sliced (optional)

Extra-virgin olive oil for serving

Flaky salt for serving

Instructions

1. **To make the broth:** Combine the tomato water, salt, and olive oil in a small bowl. Refrigerate until needed.

2. **To make the salad:** Cut the watermelon into thin, bite-size slices until you have 4 cups. Cut the cucumbers into bite-size slices. Cut the tomatoes into wedges, slices, or halves if small.

3. Arrange the tomatoes, cucumbers, and watermelon in shallow bowls. Pour the tomato broth over top, and then sprinkle with the herbs and jalapeño (if using). Drizzle with olive oil, sprinkle with flaky salt, and serve.

As you slice those beautiful heirlooms (like for the Heirloom Tomato Tart on page 57), you'll inevitably end up with end slices that aren't usable. Stash them in the freezer to make the tomato water for this soup.

VEG FORWARD

VEG FORWARD

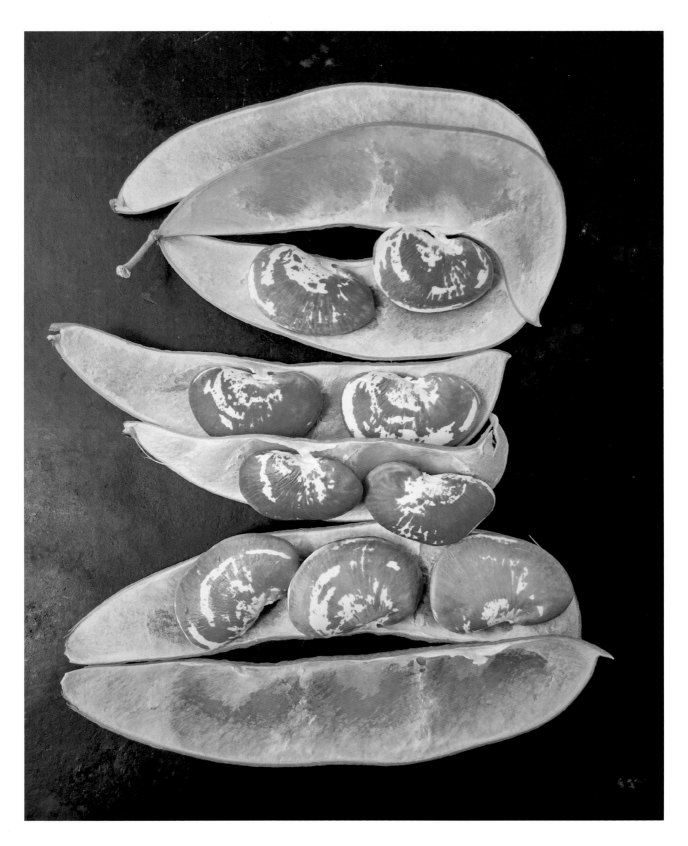

SERVES 4 GENEROUSLY

END OF SUMMER VEGETABLE SOUP

This hearty main-course soup, with sausage, beans, and lots of vegetables, is meant to be made and eaten right away, so the vegetables retain some crunch and their individual flavors. Fresh shell beans of all kinds proliferate in my farmers' market from late summer all the way through fall. They are as convenient as canned beans because they cook in about 20 minutes. Cranberry beans, whose pods and beans are a mottled hot pink, are the most common type and can be found in some specialty stores. If you can't get your hands on them, use drained, rinsed canned beans, but add them near the end of cooking time so they don't turn to mush.

For the beans

1 cup fresh shell beans, like cranberry beans, or 1 (15.5-ounce) can white beans, drained and rinsed

2 to 3 garlic cloves, slightly crushed

A few sprigs of fresh thyme

1/2 teaspoon kosher salt

4 cups water

Olive oil

For the soup

1 tablespoon olive oil, plus more for serving

1 celery stalk

3 to 4 thin carrots

Kosher salt and freshly ground pepper

1 link sweet Italian sausage (optional)

1 large or 2 small leeks, halved lengthwise, sliced, and well washed (about 1 cup)

Big handful of Romano beans, trimmed and cut into bite-size pieces

Handful of string beans, trimmed and cut into bite-size pieces

2 small or 1 medium zucchini, trimmed and cut into bite-size pieces

1 ear corn, kernels cut from cob (about 3/4 cup)

1 Parmesan rind (optional)

1/3 cup short pasta, like tubettini or ditalini

Grated Parmesan for serving

Fresh soft herbs for serving

Instructions

1. **To prepare the beans:** In a medium saucepan, combine the shell beans (if using canned white beans, you will add them later) with the garlic, thyme, salt, water, and a drizzle of olive oil. Bring to a boil, lower the heat to a bare simmer, and cook for about 20 minutes, until the beans are just tender. Let them cool a bit in the liquid while you prepare the soup.

2. **To make the soup:** Heat the oil in a small Dutch oven or large saucepan over medium heat and add the celery and carrots. Season with salt and pepper and cook for 5 minutes, or until they start to soften. Add the sausage (if using) and cook until no longer pink, about 5 minutes. Add the leeks and cook until wilted, 3 to 4 minutes.

3. Add the Romano beans, string beans, zucchini, corn, Parmesan rind (if using), and the cooked shell beans, garlic, and all the bean liquid. Discard the thyme sprigs and smash the garlic cloves against the side of the pan to dissolve them. The vegetables should be "swimming" a bit in the liquid, so add more water now if necessary. A spoon should move freely through the liquid. Bring to a boil, add the pasta and the canned beans (if using), stir well, and cook at a brisk simmer for about 10 minutes, or until the pasta is al dente. Adjust the seasonings.

4. Ladle into bowls, top with Parmesan and fresh herbs, and drizzle a little olive oil onto each serving.

If you don't plan to eat the soup right away, it's better to cook the pasta on the side and add to each portion, as it will soak up all the liquid if you let it sit in the fridge.

If you have any kind of green pesto in the fridge, swirl some into each bowl to amp up the fresh flavor even more.

Romano beans are lovely here, when you can find them, but any kind of string bean or wax bean works fine.

Yellow summer squash can be used instead of or in addition to the zucchini.

VEG FORWARD

89

INSIDE-OUT TOMATO SANDWICH
WITH HERB SALAD

Is it a sandwich or is it a salad? Hmmm, you decide. When fat, juicy heirlooms are in season, try sandwiching toasted (or grilled) bread in between the tomatoes, instead of the other way around. The bread will soak up the tomato juices, becoming soggy in the most delicious way. This is a dish you'll want to assemble on individual plates to show off the beauty of the tomatoes and stack everything up just right.

Ingredients

3 assorted tomatoes, preferably heirlooms, sliced

4 small slices sourdough or ciabatta, toasted or grilled

1 cup fresh soft herbs, like snipped chives, basil, and parsley leaves

High-quality balsamic vinegar

Extra-virgin olive oil

Flaky salt and freshly ground pepper

Instructions

1. Divide the larger tomato slices among four plates. Top with a slice of bread. Top the bread with the remaining tomato slices, scattering some of them on the plate.

2. Toss the herbs with balsamic, olive oil, salt, and pepper and top each plate with a quarter of the herb salad. Drizzle a little more vinegar and oil over each plate, and season with more salt and pepper if desired. Serve immediately.

VEG FORWARD

SERVES 4

GRILLED THREE-BEAN SALAD WITH CHARRED TOMATO VINAIGRETTE

This is not your grandma's three-bean salad, but it is inspired loosely by it. It's made entirely on the grill, so you'll need a grill platter and/or a grill basket or grill wok (see page xix). The chickpeas are crisped up in a basket, the string beans and wax beans are quickly charred, and the dressing is made simply but deliciously with grill-charred cherry tomatoes.

Ingredients

1 (15- to 16-ounce) can chickpeas, drained, rinsed, and patted dry

2 1/2 tablespoons olive oil, divided

1/2 pound string beans, stem ends trimmed

1/2 pound wax (yellow) beans, stem ends trimmed

1 large shallot, thinly sliced

Handful of Italian parsley leaves

Charred Tomato Vinaigrette (page 225)

Kosher salt and freshly ground pepper

Instructions

1. Preheat a gas grill to medium-high, then turn the burners down to low. Toss the chickpeas with 1 tablespoon of the oil and place in a grill basket or grill wok. Cook for 20 to 25 minutes, tossing occasionally, until crispy and spotted with brown. Transfer to a bowl and set aside.

2. Meanwhile, toss the green and yellow beans with 1 1/2 tablespoons of the oil and put them on a grill platter or a piece of heavy-duty foil with holes poked in it, tossing once or twice, for 3 to 4 minutes, or until lightly charred.

3. Combine the chickpeas, beans, shallot, parsley leaves, and tomato vinaigrette in a serving bowl and toss to combine. Season with salt and pepper.

To roast the chickpeas in the oven: Heat oven to 450° F. Follow the prep instructions above. Bake on a rimmed baking sheet on middle rack of oven for 30 minutes, shaking pan halfway through cooking time. Chickpeas will be very crispy, with some brown spots.

To roast the string beans in the oven: Heat oven to 450° F. Follow the prep instructions above and bake on a rimmed baking sheet on middle rack of oven for 15 to 18 minutes, tossing once until spotted with brown.

VEG FORWARD

95

VEG FORWARD

SERVES 4 AS A MAIN, 6 TO 8 AS A SIDE

NIÇOISE SPOON SALAD

Niçoise salads make frequent visits to my table in the summer, but usually in the traditional composed way, with everything arranged in sections on a large platter. This vegetarian version (if you leave out the anchovies in the dressing) is meant to be spooned out, making it a perfect portable picnic salad. Or use it as a base for an oil-poached fresh tuna, warm or cold grilled swordfish, or the traditional canned tuna.

For the dressing

3 tablespoons red wine vinegar

1 tablespoon lemon juice

1 tablespoon tapenade

3 finely chopped anchovies or 1 1/2 teaspoons anchovy paste

1 large garlic clove, grated on a Microplane

1 small shallot, finely minced

Kosher salt and freshly ground pepper

2 tablespoons vegetable oil

6 tablespoons extra-virgin olive oil

For the salad

1 pound potatoes, preferably small, waxy ones, left whole

Kosher salt and freshly ground pepper

4 large eggs, cold from the fridge

1 pound fresh beans like string beans, wax beans, or Romano beans, stem ends trimmed

1/2 cup pitted Kalamata olives, torn in half

2 tablespoons capers, rinsed

1 cup cooked or canned beans, drained

10 to 12 cooked or canned baby artichokes

1 heaping cup halved cherry tomatoes

Handful of soft herbs to garnish, such as fennel, chives, tarragon, and parsley

Instructions

1. **To make the dressing:** Combine the vinegar, lemon juice, tapenade, anchovies or paste, garlic, shallots, and salt and pepper to taste in a small bowl or jar and mix well to combine. Whisk in the oils gradually (if using a bowl) or add to the jar and shake well to emulsify. Set aside.

2. **To make the salad:** Put the potatoes in a large saucepan, add 1 teaspoon salt, and cover with cold water by 2 to 3 inches. Cook until the tip of a paring knife easily slides into the potatoes, 12 to 18 minutes.

3. As soon as the potatoes are cool enough to handle, cut them into halves or quarters and toss with 2 tablespoons of the dressing and season with salt and pepper to taste. Set aside while you prepare the rest of the salad.

4. Place the eggs in a small saucepan and cover with cold water. Add a big pinch of salt and bring to a boil over medium-high heat. Boil for 1 minute and turn off the heat. Let sit for 8 minutes, then drain and cover with cold water. Peel and quarter the eggs.

5. Use the same pot to cook the beans. Fill it with water and bring to a rolling boil. Add 1/2 teaspoon salt and the beans. Return to a boil and cook for 1 to 2 minutes, until evenly bright green. Transfer with tongs or a slotted spoon to a bowl of ice water and let sit until cool. Remove to a colander and then pat dry on paper towels. Cut into bite-size pieces.

6. Toss the potatoes, beans, olives, capers, artichokes, tomatoes, and herbs together in a serving bowl and dress with enough of the dressing to lightly coat everything. Serve any extra dressing on the side, along with the eggs.

VEG FORWARD

VEG FORWARD

SERVES 4

TRIPLE-SESAME STRING BEANS

This recipe was inspired by the delicious sesame sauce for *goma-ae*, the simple Japanese side of cold spinach (or another vegetable). I've added multiple ingredients to make it saucier and sesame-er. Though tahini is not generally used in Japanese cooking, it's right at home here, reinforcing the other sesame notes in the sauce, and adding creaminess. Slicing green beans lengthwise (Frenching them) makes them supple like noodles, and exposes more surface area so they readily absorb the flavors of the sauce.

Ingredients

2 teaspoons kosher salt

12 ounces green beans, trimmed

2 tablespoons sesame seeds, preferably unhulled, plus 2 teaspoons more for garnish

1 1/2 teaspoons sugar, preferably superfine

2 tablespoons low-sodium soy sauce or more to taste

1 tablespoon unseasoned rice wine vinegar

2 tablespoons tahini

1 tablespoon white miso

1 tablespoon dark sesame oil

1 tablespoon water

Big handful fresh shiso, basil, or mint, shredded (about 1/2 cup)

Flaky salt

Instructions

1. Bring a large saucepan of water to a boil and add the salt. Drop the green beans into the pot, return to a boil, and cook for 1 to 2 minutes until bright green. Drain and refresh in a bowl of ice water. When cool, drain again and pat dry on a double thickness of paper towels. Cut each bean in half lengthwise. They don't have to be perfect, and don't bother slicing any tiny ones. Set aside.

2. Heat a small skillet over medium heat. Add the sesame seeds and toast, tossing frequently until a shade darker and smelling toasty, 2 to 3 minutes. Set aside 2 teaspoons for the garnish.

3. Transfer to a bowl to cool slightly, then use a food processor (preferably a mini one) or a mortar and pestle to grind the seeds to a coarse powder (it should retain some texture). Return the seeds to the bowl and mix in the sugar, soy sauce, vinegar, tahini, miso, sesame oil, and water.

4. Pour the dressing over the green beans just before serving. Toss in the herbs and sprinkle flaky salt and the reserved sesame seeds over top.

You can use sugar snap peas, either in combination with string beans or on their own. Sliver them lengthwise before cooking until they turn bright green, which will take only about 10 seconds.

If you want to prep this salad ahead of time, cook the beans as directed and refrigerate, wrapped in paper towels, until ready to serve, and make the sauce too. Combine the beans, sauce, and herbs just before serving.

VEG FORWARD

VEG FORWARD

SERVES 6 TO 8

RADICCHIO, ENDIVE, AND QUINOA SALAD WITH ROASTED CHERRIES

Studded with roasted sweet cherries, this ruby-hued salad holds up well at a potluck or buffet. The radicchio, its bitterness balanced by the sweetness of the balsamic and the fruit, is sturdy enough not to wilt, and the quinoa absorbs the dressing nicely, making the salad both easy to eat and easy to serve.

For the roasted cherries

1 Fresno or small jalapeño chili

8 ounces sweet cherries, halved and pitted (about 1 1/2 cups)

1 small shallot, thinly sliced into rings (about 1/2 cup)

1 tablespoon extra-virgin olive oil

1 tablespoon high-quality balsamic vinegar

For the salad

2/3 cup/64 g walnut halves

12 ounces radicchio, cored, quartered, and thinly sliced (6 cups)

3 tablespoons extra-virgin olive oil

1 tablespoon high-quality balsamic vinegar

Kosher salt and freshly ground pepper

2 cups cooked red quinoa (from 1/2 cup dry, cooked in 1 cup water)

2 heads red Belgian endive, or 1 head white, leaves separated

4 ounces soft goat cheese, crumbled

Instructions

1. **To make the roasted cherries:** Cut the top off the chili and use a small paring knife to remove the seeds. Rinse to get all the seeds out, then slice thinly into rings.

2. Combine the chili, cherries, shallot, and olive oil in a medium cast-iron skillet. Cook on medium-high heat for 8 to 10 minutes, until the shallot is wilted and the cherries are starting to collapse. Remove from the heat and stir in the vinegar. Let cool.

3. **To make the salad:** Place the walnuts on a baking sheet and toast in a 425°F oven for 5 minutes. Let cool.

4. Place the radicchio, olive oil, vinegar, and salt and pepper to taste in a large bowl and massage with your hands to coat the radicchio with the dressing and soften it slightly. Stir in the quinoa. Toss in the endive leaves. Transfer to a serving platter or bowl and top with the cherries, goat cheese, and walnuts.

You can also roast the cherries in a 425°F oven for 18 to 20 minutes.

Red quinoa looks great with the other colors in the salad, but any color works. If you can't find red, use tricolor for a similar effect.

SERVES 4

DOUBLE-BUCKWHEAT NOODLE SALAD WITH GREEN BEANS AND BROCCOLINI

In this versatile salad, buckwheat groats echo the buckwheat in the soba noodles, adding an emphatic nuttiness and unexpected crunch. The salad is studded with green: cooked string beans, sliced lengthwise to make them more supple; raw broccolini, which softens a bit in the dressing; scallions; and fresh herbs. Feel free to change up the vegetables according to what's in season; use sugar snap peas instead of or in addition to the green beans, add some julienned carrots or cucumber, or even thinly sliced mushrooms.

For the crispy buckwheat

2 teaspoons vegetable oil

1/4 cup whole kasha (buckwheat groats)

Kosher salt

For the salad

4 ounces string beans

8 ounces soba noodles

2 tablespoons sesame oil

2 tablespoons low-sodium soy sauce

1 tablespoon unseasoned rice wine vinegar

Kosher salt

8 small spring onions or scallions, thinly sliced (scant 1/2 cup)

3 ounces broccolini or purple sprouting broccoli, trimmed and chopped (about 1 cup)

1/2 cup lightly packed herbs, such as Thai basil, basil, mint, or cilantro

1 tablespoon chili crisp, or more to taste

Instructions

1. **To make the crispy buckwheat:** Heat the oil in a small saucepan over medium heat. Add the kasha and stir to coat evenly in the oil. Lower the heat once the kasha starts to sizzle. Cook until it smells nutty and turns a shade darker, 6 to 8 minutes. Transfer to a bowl. Salt to taste and set aside.

2. **To make the salad:** Fill a large pot with salted water and bring to a boil. Fill a large bowl with ice water.

3. Cook the string beans for 1 minute, drain, refresh in ice water, then drain again. Pat dry on paper towels. Trim the ends off the beans and slice in half lengthwise.

4. In the same pot you cooked the string beans in, cook the soba noodles according to the package directions. Drain and rinse with cold water, then drain well.

5. Toss the noodles with sesame oil, soy sauce, vinegar, and salt to taste. Add the string beans, spring onions, and broccoli or broccolini and toss to combine. Top with the herbs, buckwheat, and chili crisp and serve.

The amount of chili crisp is up to you and will depend somewhat on its heat level. You can use Salsa Macha (page 214) instead of chili crisp, if you'd like.

VEG FORWARD

103

SERVES 4 TO 6

GRILLED SAVOY CABBAGE WEDGES WITH SPICY THAI-INSPIRED DRESSING

Cabbage makes a brief visit to a hot grill, where it takes on a slightly smoky flavor and some crunch. I serve it with a steak knife and fork. Savoy cabbage has a softer texture and milder flavor than ordinary cabbage. Don't be afraid to use the amount of fish sauce called for—it's essential to the well-balanced dressing.

For the dressing

1 tablespoon lime juice

1 tablespoon light brown sugar

2 tablespoons rice wine vinegar

1 tablespoon fish sauce or Yondu

1 tablespoon chili garlic sauce or sriracha, plus more to taste

2 tablespoons vegetable oil

Freshly ground pepper

For the cabbage

1 head Savoy cabbage (1 1/2 to 2 pounds)

1 1/2 tablespoons vegetable oil

Kosher salt

1 cup loosely packed mint leaves

Big handful cilantro sprigs

2 scallions, thinly sliced

1/4 cup salted peanuts, lightly crushed

Instructions

1. **To make the dressing:** Blend the lime juice, brown sugar, vinegar, fish sauce, and chili garlic sauce or sriracha in a small bowl with a fork. Blend in the oil and pepper and set aside.

2. **To grill the cabbage:** Trim any wilted or torn outer leaves. Trim the bottom of the stem to remove the brown portion, but leave the stem and core intact so the wedges hold together on the grill.

3. Cut the head in half, wash well, and pat dry. Then cut each half into 4 wedges, for a total of 8 wedges. Spread out on a baking sheet and coat on all sides with the oil, then sprinkle lightly with salt.

4. Heat a gas or charcoal grill to medium-high. Grill the cabbage wedges for 2 to 3 minutes on each side until lightly charred on the edges and surfaces.

5. Arrange the cabbage wedges on a platter and drizzle with the dressing. Roughly chop most of the mint, reserving a handful of whole leaves for garnish. Top with the mint and cilantro and sprinkle with the scallions and peanuts.

You can roast the cabbage instead of grilling it; cook at 500°F for 12 minutes on an oiled baking sheet, turning wedges over halfway through cooking time until charred on the edges and softened but still crunchy.

You can shred the cabbage and mix with the dressing for a more slaw-like presentation.

Use as much of the chili garlic sauce or sriracha as you like; don't be afraid to go spicy.

VEG FORWARD

VEG FORWARD

SERVES 4 TO 6

SMOKY CORN SALAD

Colorful corn salad in a creamy yogurt-based dressing gets a hint of smokiness from grilled corn, jalapeño, and scallions. A touch of smoked paprika brings in another layer of smoky flavor. This is one of those salads that can sit for a while with no deterioration or wilting thanks to the sturdiness of the kale.

Ingredients

4 large ears corn, husked

2 tablespoons unsalted butter

1 jalapeño

12 scallions, trimmed

3/4 cup Greek yogurt

2 tablespoons lime juice

1/2 cup roughly chopped cilantro

Kosher salt and freshly ground pepper

2 cups shredded lacinato kale (stripped from the stems of about 6 large leaves)

1 pint cherry tomatoes, halved or quartered if large

2 to 3 ounces feta

1/2 teaspoon smoked paprika, plus more for finishing

Instructions

1. Heat a grill to medium-high. Wrap 2 ears of corn and 1 tablespoon butter in a snug packet with heavy-duty foil. Repeat with the other 2 ears.

2. Place the foil-wrapped corn directly on the grill and cook for 5 to 6 minutes on each side. Place the jalapeño on a cooler spot on the grill and cook for about 8 minutes, turning to brown evenly. Open one of the corn packets to make sure the corn is caramelized and brown; if not, turn the heat to high and grill for another 2 minutes on each side. Remove from the grill, open the foil packets, and let the corn cool somewhat.

3. Lay the scallions perpendicular to the grill grates and cook for 1 to 2 minutes on each side, until charred. Cut into 1-inch lengths. Set aside. Finely chop the jalapeño, leaving the seeds behind.

4. Using a sharp knife, cut the kernels from the cob into a bowl.

5. Whisk the yogurt, lime juice, and cilantro in a small bowl. Season with salt and pepper to taste. Add the chopped jalapeño a little at a time, tasting as you go to get the right heat level.

6. Add the kale, half the scallions, half the tomatoes, half the feta, the smoked paprika, and the dressing to the bowl and toss to combine thoroughly. Season with salt and pepper to taste.

7. Transfer to a serving bowl and top with the remaining tomatoes, scallions, and feta. Generously sprinkle smoked paprika over top and serve.

VEG FORWARD

KERNELS WITHOUT THE CLEANUP

To cut corn from the cob, use a large, shallow wooden salad bowl. The bowl catches any errant corn kernels, which otherwise tend to fly around the room, and makes for a gentle landing for your knife. Stand the cob on end (trimming it at the base if necessary to make a stable surface) and cut straight down with your knife as close to the cob as possible to remove the kernels.

SERVES 4 TO 6

ZUCCHINI CARPACCIO

Stash this recipe in your back pocket for when the zucchini just keep coming. Delightfully simple, it's dazzling to look at, yet there's barely anything to cook, except for the dukkah, a blend of seeds and spices that adds flavor and crunch. And if you do have zucchini in your garden, take advantage of their beautiful blossoms to garnish the dish.

Ingredients

3 medium yellow and/or green zucchini, about 8 ounces each

1 tablespoon lemon juice

2 tablespoons extra-virgin olive oil

Kosher salt and freshly ground pepper

1 ear fresh corn, kernels cut from the cob

1/4 cup chopped mint

1/4 cup chopped dill

2 to 3 zucchini blossoms, stamens removed (optional)

For the seedy dukkah

1 tablespoon olive oil

1/2 cup raw pepitas

1/4 cup sunflower seeds

1 tablespoon cumin seeds

2 tablespoons sesame seeds

3/4 teaspoon flaky sea salt such as Maldon

Aleppo-style pepper or freshly ground pepper

Instructions

1. Slice the zucchini as thinly as possible, about 1/8-inch thick, with a very sharp knife or with a mandoline. Arrange the slices on a large platter, spreading them out so they are in an overlapping single layer.

2. Drizzle with the lemon juice and olive oil and sprinkle lightly and evenly with salt and pepper. Top with the corn, mint, dill, and dukkah. Tear the zucchini blossoms (if using) into strips and scatter them over the top.

3. Let sit at room temperature for about 30 minutes to let the zucchini soften before serving.

4. **To make the dukkah:** Heat a small skillet over medium heat. Heat the oil and add the pepitas and sunflower seeds. Toast until golden, stirring frequently, about 8 minutes.

5. Scoop the seeds onto a plate, leaving the oil in the pan. Add the cumin and sesame seeds and toast until fragrant, about 3 minutes. Add the salt and pepper to taste. Grind coarsely using a mortar and pestle or spice grinder and store in an airtight container for up to several weeks.

Shaved Parmesan gives another layer of flavor; add it after the dukkah.

Harvest only the male blooms, which will be attached to a short, slender stem, not at the end of a zucchini. This way the plant will continue to produce squash.

VEG FORWARD

GRILLED ZUCCHINI WITH WHIPPED RICOTTA, CALABRIAN CHILI, AND ALMONDS

This is one of those dishes that is way more than the sum of its parts. Each element is easy to prepare, leaving only last-minute assembly. Tender, baby zucchini nestle into creamy whipped ricotta and are topped with roasted almonds and a drizzle of Calabrian chilies.

For the zucchini

8 baby zucchini (2 pounds), sliced in half lengthwise and scored

Kosher salt and freshly ground pepper

1 ½ tablespoons olive oil

For the chili oil

1 tablespoon Calabrian chilies (paste or finely chopped jarred)

1 ½ tablespoons olive oil

For the whipped ricotta

1 cup ricotta

1 tablespoon milk, or more as needed

Drizzle of olive oil

¼ teaspoon kosher salt

For the almonds

1 tablespoon olive oil

½ cup whole raw almonds, very coarsely chopped

½ cup loosely packed herbs, such as mint and basil, some chopped and some leaves left whole

Flaky salt

Instructions

1. **To prep the zucchini:** Sprinkle the zucchini evenly with salt and pepper, then drizzle with olive oil to coat. Set aside.

2. **To make the chili oil:** Stir together the Calabrian chilies and olive oil in a small bowl and set aside.

3. **To make the whipped ricotta:** Combine the ricotta, milk, olive oil, and salt in a food processor and process until smooth. Set aside. Add more milk if necessary if the ricotta is too thick, until it looks like spreadable frosting.

4. **To toast the almonds:** Place a small skillet over medium-low heat. Add the olive oil and almonds to the pan and cook until golden brown, 4 to 6 minutes. Drain on paper towels and sprinkle with flaky salt. Set aside.

5. **To grill the zucchini:** Grill the zucchini over a medium fire, starting with the cut side down, for 2 to 3 minutes per side, until they're seared with grill marks and look softer and juicy.

6. **To assemble:** Spread the whipped ricotta on a large platter. Top with zucchini, then drizzle with the chili oil and sprinkle with almonds and herbs. Season with flaky salt and black pepper to taste. Serve warm or at room temperature.

Baby zucchini, about 6 inches long, work especially well here, but if you can't find those, use the smallest ones you can find with the firmest texture and the fewest seeds. If you only have larger ones, split them in half lengthwise and grill for as long as it takes to get the flesh softened and juicy and nicely marked by the grill. Cut into smaller pieces for serving.

Calabrian chili paste is increasingly available and has a tingly kind of heat, but you can use sriracha or even a loose harissa sauce instead.

To roast the zucchini in the oven instead, place them cut sides down on a baking sheet and cook for 15 to 20 minutes at 450°F.

SERVES 4 TO 6

BUTTER-STEAMED POTATOES

You may have never thought of cooking potatoes this way. They're not roasted. Not boiled. Not fried. Instead, they're simply steamed in a covered pot, with only the butter and the potatoes themselves providing the moisture. Small potatoes, ranging from marble to golf ball size, work best here, but bigger ones will work too. The potatoes become nutty tasting as the butter browns along with the skins, and all of the natural potato flavor is locked in.

Ingredients

2 tablespoons butter

2 pounds new potatoes, scrubbed

6 whole garlic cloves, peeled

1/2 teaspoon kosher salt and freshly ground pepper

Flaky salt

A handful of roughly chopped fresh herbs, like tarragon and dill

Instructions

1. Heat a wide covered saucepan or Dutch oven over medium to medium-low heat. Add the butter and cook until melted.

2. Add the potatoes and garlic, and add salt and pepper to taste. Cover and cook, stirring or shaking occasionally, until golden brown and a paring knife slides into a potato with no resistance, about 20 minutes. Adjust heat as needed to avoid burning the butter or garlic. Sprinkle with flaky salt, scatter the herbs on top, and serve immediately.

VEG FORWARD

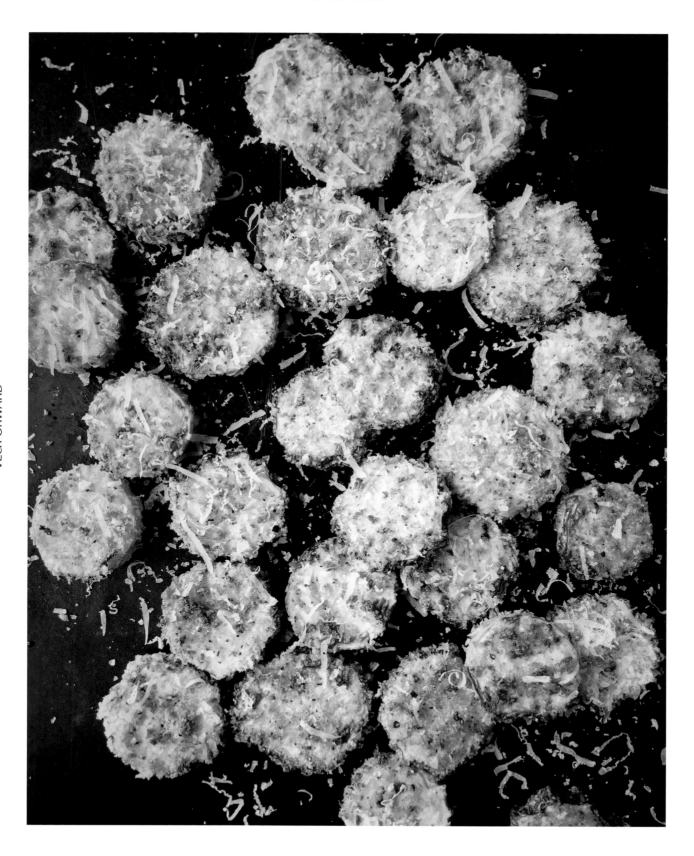

SERVES 4 AS A SNACK OR A SIDE

AIR-FRIED ZUCCHINI

My husband and I each have fond memories of being served battered and fried zucchini in old-school Italian restaurants. This recipe is healthier, easier, and satisfies those cravings. I pretty much never deep-fry at home, partly due to the mess it creates, and because I don't eat much fried food. When I want something that seems fried, I pull out the air fryer. You'll need to cook the zucchini slices in single-layer batches so that they brown and cook evenly, but at the end, you can pile them up and reheat all the batches together in the air fryer and they will re-crisp as they warm up.

Ingredients

1 1/4 cups panko breadcrumbs

Scant 2/3 cup grated Parmesan cheese, plus more for garnish

1/2 to 3/4 teaspoon Aleppo-style pepper (depending on how spicy you like things)

1/2 teaspoon kosher salt

1/4 teaspoon freshly ground pepper

1/2 cup buttermilk

2 tablespoons plain yogurt (any kind)

2 medium zucchini (about 12 ounces), cut into 1/4-inch thick rounds

Olive oil spray

Instructions

1. Heat the air fryer to 375°F. Mix together the panko, Parmesan, red pepper, salt, and black pepper on a dinner plate and set aside.

2. Mix the buttermilk and yogurt in a shallow bowl until smooth and add the zucchini slices. Use a rubber spatula to mix well, making sure the pieces are well-coated.

3. Remove the zucchini slices one at a time, letting the excess drip off, and place them on the panko mixture. Turn them and press down gently to adhere the crumbs on both sides.

4. Carefully arrange the slices in the air fryer basket in a single layer, being careful not to knock off the coating. Spray with olive oil. Fry for about 10 minutes, until golden and crispy. Using tongs, transfer the zucchini to a serving plate. Serve in batches with drinks or continue frying until all the zucchini are cooked. You can keep the zucchini warm in the oven or reheat all at once in the air fryer, which will re-crisp the slices. Grate more Parmesan over top before serving hot.

To make these in the oven, you'll need to have a convection setting. Heat the oven to 400°F convection. Line a baking sheet with foil, spray the foil with olive oil spray, and spread the zucchini slices out evenly. Spray the tops of the zucchini slices. Cook for 30 minutes, turning once.

The size of the zucchini doesn't matter much. You can use 1 large or 2 small or anything in between.

VEG FORWARD

MAKES 1 LOAF; SERVES 8 TO 10

CHOCOLATE ZUCCHINI BREAD

More is more with this moist winner of a zucchini bread, made with olive oil and cocoa and crammed with nuts, raisins, and chocolate chips. Gently squeeze the grated zucchini, but don't go crazy. A big part of what makes the bread so good is that moisture.

Ingredients

1 (12-ounce) zucchini, grated on the large holes of a box grater (about 2 ¹/₂ cups)

1¹/₂ cups plus 2 tablespoons/200g all-purpose flour

¹/₃ cup/39 g Dutch-process cocoa

¹/₂ teaspoon ground cinnamon

¹/₂ teaspoon ground ginger

³/₄ teaspoon kosher salt

³/₄ teaspoon baking powder

³/₄ teaspoon baking soda

2 large eggs

¹/₂ cup olive oil

¹/₄ cup sour cream or yogurt (any kind)

¹/₂ cup/101 g granulated sugar

¹/₂ cup/110 g light brown sugar

1 teaspoon vanilla extract

³/₄ cup/75 g walnuts, coarsely chopped

³/₄ cup/120 g semisweet chocolate morsels

¹/₂ cup/75 g raisins

1¹/₂ tablespoons raw sugar

Instructions

1. Heat the oven to 350°F. Spray a standard 8-by-4-inch loaf pan with cooking spray or use soft butter to grease the pan. Make a parchment sling by cutting parchment paper to fit the length of the loaf pan, keeping 2 inches of overhang on the long sides for handles.

2. Place the zucchini in a sieve or colander and press down to extract the excess liquid. Turn a few times and repeat. Set aside to drain while you assemble the cake.

3. Set a sieve over a medium bowl and add the flour, cocoa, cinnamon, ginger, salt, baking powder, and baking soda. Use a spoon to stir the mixture and help it sift through the sieve. Set aside.

4. In a separate, smaller bowl, combine the eggs, olive oil, sour cream, both sugars, and vanilla. Whisk until smooth. Pour it into the bowl with the dry mixture and whisk until mostly incorporated.

5. Switch to a rubber spatula and fold in the zucchini, walnuts, chocolate morsels, and raisins. Be sure to scrape the bottom of the bowl and make sure everything is well incorporated. Scrape the mixture into the pan, even the top, and sprinkle with the raw sugar.

6. Bake for 70 to 75 minutes, until a wooden skewer comes out mostly clean. There may be some crumbs clinging to the skewer, but the cake shouldn't be wet. If you're unsure, bake for 5 minutes longer.

7. Run a butter knife along the short ends of the pan (where there's no paper) and let cool in the pan for 10 to 15 minutes. Use the paper to lift the cake from the pan and set on a wire rack to cool completely (or for as long as you can stand to wait).

While it might be tempting to use that giant zucchini that has stayed too long in the garden for this quick bread, it is is not the best choice, since it will have developed seeds. If it has, simply cut the four sides off and discard the seedy center, then grate the zucchini.

A little more or a little less zucchini won't throw off the recipe, but don't add too much or the pan might overflow.

It's always a good idea to place a parchment or foil-lined sheet pan under the pan. Not only does this make it easier to turn and remove it from the oven, but it will catch any spills should they happen.

VEG FORWARD

MAKES ONE 12-INCH GALETTE; SERVES 8

PEACH AND ALMOND GALETTE

Whether you call them galettes or crostatas, these free-form tarts are the simplest and most beautiful way to showcase summer fruit, and they're a lot less fussy than a pie. Rolling the dough on a sheet of parchment and transferring it to an iron skillet ensures that all the juices will be contained within the pan when the tart bakes. Those that do break through the dough will caramelize but not burn, making the edges something to fight over.

For the crust

2 cups/256 g all-purpose flour

3/4 teaspoon kosher salt

1 tablespoon granulated sugar

1/4 cup/24 g sliced almonds

14 tablespoons/198 g (1 3/4 sticks) ice-cold unsalted butter, cut into 1/2-inch slices

1/4 cup/59 ml ice water, plus more if needed

For the filling

2 pounds (6 to 8) peaches, ripe but firm

1/2 cup/101 g granulated sugar

1/4 cup/32 g all-purpose flour

For baking

1/4 cup/24 g sliced almonds

2 tablespoons granulated sugar

1 teaspoon unsalted butter

Instructions

1. **To make the crust:** Combine the flour, salt, sugar, and almonds in a food processor; pulse until combined. Add the butter and pulse until the largest pieces are the size of walnut halves. Transfer to a wide bowl and squeeze the butter pieces, flattening them between your fingers. Sprinkle the ice water over the flour mixture and mix it in evenly, tossing with a fork. If there are a lot of loose, dry crumbs at the bottom of the bowl and it won't hold together when squeezed, add more ice water, 1 tablespoon at a time.

2. Press the dough together, gathering up any dry bits until the dough forms a shaggy, cohesive mass. Transfer to a sheet of plastic wrap. Wrap and press into a flat, round disk. Shape the edges with your hands so they are not crumbly. Chill until firm, at least 1 hour and preferably 2, and as long as 2 days. Or freeze for up to 3 months.

3. Heat the oven to 400°F, with a rack in the middle. Let the dough soften slightly at room temperature until it's malleable enough to roll out. On a lightly floured piece of parchment paper about 18 inches long, roll the dough out into a circle roughly 15 inches in diameter and 1/8 to 1/4 inch thick. It may hang over on the short sides.

4. Lift the parchment by opposite corners and transfer to a large (12-inch) cast-iron skillet or another ovenproof skillet, fitting the parchment and dough into the pan. Refrigerate for about 15 minutes.

5. **Meanwhile, make the filling:** Cut the peaches into 6 or 8 wedges each and toss with the sugar. Sprinkle the flour on the dough, evenly covering the bottom of the dough-lined pan. Tumble the peaches into the dough and fold the dough over all around to enclose the filling. Refrigerate again until firm, 15 to 30 minutes.

6. Brush the crust with cold water and sprinkle with the almonds. Sprinkle the sugar over the fruit and crust. Dot the filling with butter and bake for 55 to 65 minutes, or until the filling is furiously bubbling and the crust is deep golden brown.

7. Place the skillet on a cooling rack or a cool stove burner grate and let cool for at least 30 minutes to let the juices thicken. Carefully pick up the parchment by opposite corners, transfer to a serving plate, and slide out the paper (or don't). Serve the galette warm or at room temperature.

You can use any fruit, using about 2 pounds of whatever is in season, adjusting the sugar to your taste and the sweetness of the fruit. Try apricots, plums, apples, pears, berries, or a combination. In most cases, 3 to 4 tablespoons of flour is about right for thickening the fruit juices, but if your fruit mixture seems extra juicy, just add a little more. If the fruit looks soupy in the oven, don't worry—it will thicken as it cools.

VEG FORWARD

119

SERVES 6

PLUM CLAFOUTIS

The traditional fruit for clafoutis—which is essentially a pancake batter baked with fruit in it—is cherries. I like mine with tart plums, which are way easier to pit. This rendition is creamy and custardy and extremely fast to make. It works as a not-too-sweet dessert, a brunch dish, or an afternoon snack.

Ingredients

¹/₂ cup plus 2 tablespoons/126 g granulated sugar

¹/₂ cup/64 g all-purpose flour

¹/₂ teaspoon baking powder

¹/₂ teaspoon ground cardamom

Pinch of kosher salt

1 ¹/₂ cups/355 ml whole milk

2 large eggs

2 tablespoons butter, melted, plus more for dish

1 teaspoon vanilla extract

4 medium plums (about 12 ounces), pitted and sliced into 8 wedges each

2 tablespoons raw sugar

Instructions

1. Heat the oven to 400°F, with a rack in the middle. Butter a 9- to 10-inch baking dish (2 quart) and set on a baking sheet.

2. Whisk together the granulated sugar, flour, baking powder, cardamom, and salt. In a large measuring cup or small bowl, mix the milk, eggs, butter, and vanilla. Gradually add the wet mixture into the dry ingredients, whisking constantly as you go, and pour the mixture into the baking dish.

3. Scatter the plums over the batter and bake for 10 minutes. Lower the oven temperature to 375°F and bake for another 10 minutes. Remove from the oven and sprinkle the top of the clafoutis with the raw sugar and continue to bake until set, slightly puffed, and brown around the edges, an additional 30 to 35 minutes, depending on the size of the dish. Serve with a spoon while still warm, or cut into slices once cooled.

SERVES 8 TO 10

TAHINI PEACH COBBLER

Tahini adds a subtle and slightly bitter background note to an otherwise traditional Southern peach cobbler. The butter is melted in the baking dish rather than being mixed into the batter, and it surrounds the batter as it's poured into the dish, resulting in chewy edges, a cakey interior, and juicy fruit. It's hard to imagine a simpler and more perfect summer dessert.

Ingredients

4 tablespoons/57 g (1/2 stick) unsalted butter

6 to 7 large ripe peaches (about 2 pounds), sliced into 8 wedges each

1/2 cup/101 g granulated sugar, divided

1/2 cup/110 g light brown sugar

1 cup/128 g all-purpose flour

2 teaspoons baking powder

1/2 teaspoon kosher salt

Pinch of ground cardamom

1 cup whole milk

1/3 cup/80 g tahini, warmed in the microwave if necessary to liquefy

1 teaspoon vanilla extract

Vanilla ice cream for serving

Instructions

1. Heat the oven to 350°F, with a rack in the middle. Place the butter in a large (3-quart) baking dish and heat in the oven for 10 minutes.

2. Meanwhile, combine the peaches and 1/4 cup (50 g) of the granulated sugar and let sit for 10 minutes, tossing occasionally, until juicy.

3. Whisk together the remaining 1/4 cup/50 g granulated sugar, the brown sugar, flour, baking powder, salt, cardamom, milk, tahini, and vanilla. Pour into the baking dish. Scatter the peaches, along with their juices, over top and bake for 50 to 55 minutes, or until puffed and golden brown all the way to the center. Serve warm with vanilla ice cream.

VEG FORWARD

SERVES 4

GREEN VEGGIE ENCHILADAS

Stuffed full of Swiss chard, mushrooms, and black beans, these enchiladas are moistened by a zippy salsa verde, made from the tomatillos that are abundant in the fall. Creamy, tangy goat cheese and melty Monterey Jack add the requisite richness. While you can buy one of the good, jarred versions of salsa verde, they are expensive, and not as tasty as homemade. I urge you to make your own, since it's a cornerstone of this dish. You'll have about a cup of salsa left over from the recipe listed below, which comes in handy for reheating any leftovers, since the enchiladas tend to dry out as they sit and absorb moisture.

Ingredients

1 bunch green Swiss chard (about 12 ounces)

8 ounces cremini (Baby Bella) mushrooms, sliced (use 12 ounces if not using oyster mushrooms)

4 ounces oyster mushrooms, sliced (optional)

Kosher salt and freshly ground pepper

4 scallions or stalks of green garlic, sliced, divided

Tomatillo Salsa (page 223)

1 (15.5-ounce) can black beans, drained and rinsed

8 (6-inch) soft corn tortillas (ideally a corn and wheat combo, like Maria and Ricardo's or 365 by Whole Foods Market)

6 ounces soft goat cheese

4 ounces Monterey Jack cheese, grated (1 1/4 cups)

For serving

Thinly sliced radishes

Fresh cilantro leaves

Thinly sliced jalapeño (optional)

Lime wedges

Sour cream or crème fraîche

Salsa Macha (page 214; optional)

Instructions

1. Heat the oven to 375°F. Strip the chard leaves from the stems, reserving the stems. Wash and dry the stems and leaves separately and chop the stems. Tear the leaves into smaller pieces.

2. Heat a large (12-inch) skillet over high heat. Add the mushrooms and season with 1/2 teaspoon salt and some pepper. Cook for 5 to 7 minutes, tossing frequently until they release their liquid and start to caramelize. Reduce the heat to medium-high if necessary. Add the chard stems and 1 of the scallions or 1 of the green garlic stalks and cook for 2 minutes longer. Add the chard leaves and 1/2 teaspoon salt, cover, and cook for 2 minutes, opening the lid to toss once or twice. Transfer to a bowl, fold in 1/2 cup of the salsa and the beans and cool slightly.

3. Pour 1 1/2 cups of the tomatillo salsa into a large baking dish. Dip each tortilla into the salsa, coating both sides, and stack up on a lunch plate. Crumble a generous tablespoon of the goat cheese onto the center of the top tortilla, followed by 1/3 cup of the vegetable filling. Roll up the tortilla tightly, enclosing the filling, and transfer to the baking dish with the seam side down. Repeat with the remaining tortillas. If you have any leftover filling, scatter it around the edges of the dish.

4. Pour 1 more cup of tomatillo salsa over the enchiladas and around the sides. Top with the Monterey Jack cheese and the remaining 3 scallions or green garlic stalks. Spray a piece of foil with cooking spray and cover the dish tightly. Bake for 35 minutes, then remove the foil. Bake for 15 minutes longer, until bubbling at the edges and starting to brown on top. Brown the top under the broiler for 2 or 3 minutes if desired. Serve hot with the radishes, cilantro, jalapeño (if using), lime wedges, and sour cream or crème fraîche on the side. Serve with salsa macha if you have it on hand.

Besides buying jarred salsa verde (you'll need 3 cups), you can shortcut this dish by using leftover cooked veggies to bulk up or replace the filling (think roasted squash, cauliflower, mushrooms, zucchini).

You can tuck in some cooked chicken if you want.

WHICH TORTILLA?

If you use pure corn tortillas instead of soft corn tortillas, which are made with a combo of wheat and corn, they need to be fried briefly to keep them from falling apart while baking. You can use a shortcut method that creates less mess: heat the oven to 325°F, place the tortillas in a single layer on two baking sheets, brush or spray both sides with oil, and bake them for 15 minutes, turning them once. Soft corn tortillas give the dish the flavor and texture of corn without the extra step of baking or frying. Flour tortillas, while not traditional in enchiladas, will also work and don't need any preparation.

EGGPLANT PARM AND PASTA BAKE

This oven-baked dish has all the yumminess of Eggplant Parm, with the bonus of a bottom layer of pasta. I usually roast the eggplant slices, but they can also be grilled. Make sure to slice them the full 1/2 inch thick because they'll shrink a lot when cooking, and you want them to retain some heft and softness. My first choice for this dish is the streaky purple eggplant known as Graffiti—it has hardly any seeds and is smaller and has none of the bitterness of ordinary eggplant.

Ingredients

2 1/2 pounds (5 to 7) small eggplant, such as Grafitti or Italian

2 tablespoons olive oil, or more as needed

Olive oil spray, as needed

Kosher salt and freshly ground pepper

1 cup/6 ounces ditalini or tubettini pasta

Simple Chunky Tomato Sauce (page 217), divided

8 ounces ricotta, preferably fresh

8 to 10 large basil leaves

6 to 8 ounces low-moisture (not fresh) mozzarella, grated

1/2 ounce Parmesan cheese, grated (1/2 fluffy cup)

Instructions

1. Heat the oven to 425°F, with racks in the upper and lower thirds of the oven. Trim the eggplant and cut into 1/2-inch-thick rounds. Spread 1 tablespoon of the oil on a baking sheet. Spread the eggplant slices out in a single layer, spray (or brush) with olive oil, and sprinkle evenly with salt and pepper. Turn the slices and repeat on the second side. If they don't all fit, use a second baking sheet.

2. Roast for 30 to 40 minutes, turning the pan around halfway through, until the eggplant slices brown on the bottoms. Remove the pan from the oven and turn each piece of eggplant. Roast for 10 to 15 minutes more, until brown on both sides. Reduce the oven heat to 400°F.

3. Oil a large (3-quart) baking dish and pour the dry pasta into it, followed by 3 cups of the sauce. Mix well. Layer half the eggplant slices on top, leaving plenty of space between them, and dollop the ricotta all around. Tear the basil leaves and sprinkle over top. Arrange the remaining eggplant slices on top, staggering them with the first layer.

4. Add 2 cups of sauce to the top, followed by the mozzarella and Parmesan. Spray or brush a piece of foil with oil and crimp tightly onto the baking dish. Place the baking dish on a baking sheet and bake for 50 minutes, or until bubbling. Remove the foil and bake for another 20 minutes, or until brown and bubbly. Let rest for 10 minutes and serve hot.

The recipe will not use the full recipe of tomato sauce, but you may want more when serving or when reheating leftovers, since the pasta drinks up some of the moisture.

You can use your favorite jarred marinara here; use 5 cups and dilute with 1/2 cup water.

The eggplant slices may not all fit on one pan, in which case divide them between two pans and switch the positions halfway through the roasting time.

SERVES 4

CAULIFLOWER-PEPITA TACOS WITH AVOCADO CREMA

Versatile cauliflower stars as a taco filling, and crunchy pepitas add yet another layer of texture and flavor, with a cool avocado cream enfolding them. Peanutty, garlicky, chili-laced salsa macha and fresh cilantro and green chilies complete the party. I like to present everything as a spread, letting people choose what they want and make their own tacos. Homemade tortillas make it special, but of course you can buy them; choose the best ones you can find.

For the roasted cauliflower

1 1/2 pounds cauliflower (2 small or 1 large head)

2 tablespoons olive oil

1 teaspoon ground cumin

1/2 teaspoon garlic powder

3/4 teaspoon kosher salt

Freshly ground pepper

For the toasted pepitas

1/4 cup olive oil

1/4 cup pepitas

Kosher salt

For the avocado crema

1 ripe avocado, pitted, peeled, and quartered

1/4 cup sour cream or Greek yogurt

Juice of 1/2 lime

1/4 teaspoon kosher salt or to taste

Pinch of cayenne pepper

For serving

Corn tortillas, preferably homemade (page 214)

Salsa Macha (page 214)

Cilantro sprigs

Thinly sliced serrano or jalapeño chilies

Cotija or feta cheese, crumbled

Instructions

1. **To make the cauliflower:** Heat the oven to 425°F. Cut the cauliflower into florets, creating flat sides so they can caramelize better. Toss with the oil, cumin, garlic powder, salt, and pepper. Cook for 35 to 40 minutes, tossing once after 25 minutes.

2. **To make the toasted pepitas:** Heat the oil in a small skillet over medium heat until hot. Test by adding a pepita to the oil: it should start sizzling right away. Add the pepitas to the oil and cook for about 3 minutes, until golden. Scoop them out onto a paper towel–lined plate and sprinkle with salt.

3. **To make the avocado crema:** Combine the avocado with the sour cream or yogurt, lime juice, salt, and cayenne in a food processor and pulse until completely smooth, scraping once or twice.

4. If using homemade tortillas, warm them, wrapped in foil, in a 200°F oven for 15 minutes. For store-bought tortillas, heat them for a minute or two on each side in a hot skillet until they brown a bit on the edges. Keep them warm in the oven wrapped in foil.

5. Serve with the cauliflower, pepitas, avocado crema, salsa macha, cilantro, chilies, and cheese and let everyone make their own tacos.

VEG FORWARD

SERVES 4

COLLARD WRAPS WITH PINTO BEANS AND CHEESE

Collard greens are soft and flexible and stand in nicely for flour tortillas in these burrito-like wraps. The rice and cheese fill up the wrap and hold things together, but you can let your imagination run wild and change up the fillings to use what you have on hand (see notes below).

Ingredients

Kosher salt

8 large collard leaves

2 cups cooked brown rice or quinoa

1 (15.5-ounce) can pinto beans, drained and rinsed

Thinly sliced jalapeño or Fresno chili to taste

1/2 cup sliced scallions (6 small)

1/2 cup cilantro leaves

4 ounces grated cheese, such as Monterey Jack or Cheddar (about 3/4 cup)

Your favorite hot sauce or salsa

Cooking spray

Instructions

1. Fill a large, wide pot with salted water and bring to a boil. Prepare a large bowl of ice water.

2. Wash the collard leaves and remove the tough stems by cutting along both sides with the tip of a large knife until you reach about halfway up the leaf, where the stems start to thin out and are more flexible. (Do not cut the leaves in half.) This will enable you to roll up the leaf.

3. Cook the collard leaves, one at a time, in the boiling water for 10 seconds, just until bright green and softened. Immediately transfer to the ice water. Pat the leaves dry on a paper towel.

4. Lay the leaf flat on a work surface in front of you, veined side up, and overlap the two halves of the leaf where you cut the stem out to close the gap. On the lower third of the leaf, arrange 1/4 cup of the rice or quinoa, a scant 1/4 cup of the beans, a few jalapeño slices, some scallions, cilantro, 2 tablespoons of the cheese, and hot sauce to taste. Spray or brush the top end of the leaf with oil to help seal. Roll the bottom up over the filling, tuck in the sides, and continue rolling up tightly like a burrito until you reach the top. Repeat with the remaining collard leaves.

5. Cook the wraps, seam side down, in a panini press or in a nonstick skillet on medium heat until browned and just starting to leak, 3 to 4 minutes, depending how many you are cooking at once.

Add any kind of kraut (I like ruby kraut with beets) or kimchi for a different flavor.

Use leftover chopped cooked vegetables in the filling, such as broccoli, winter squash, or cauliflower.

VEG FORWARD

SERVES 4

PINKALICIOUS PASTA

The beets and hazelnuts in the vivacious kale pesto for this pasta will turn it a stunning shade of pink. It's gorgeous and special enough for a dinner party but also weeknight-friendly if you've made the pesto ahead of time, since all you need to do to get it on the table is boil the pasta and heat it through with the pasta. You can roast the beets and blanch the kale ahead of time, whizzing up the pesto at the last minute, or make it completely ahead of time.

Ingredients

1 medium beet (about 6 ounces), trimmed, peeled, and quartered

3 garlic cloves, smashed

3 tablespoons extra-virgin olive oil, plus more as needed

Kosher salt and freshly ground pepper

3 ounces (heaping ½ cup) raw hazelnuts

3 ounces (½ bunch) dinosaur kale, stemmed

½ cup grated pecorino or Parmesan cheese (3/4 ounce), plus more for serving

Pinch of red pepper flakes

1 pound rigatoni

1 watermelon radish for serving (optional)

Instructions

1. Heat the oven to 400°F. Lay a piece of foil on a small baking sheet and place the beet and garlic on top. Drizzle with enough olive oil to lightly coat, and season with salt and pepper. Gather the foil into a pouch, sealing it well to trap the steam, and place the pan in the oven. Roast for 30 to 40 minutes, until the beet shows no resistance to the tip of a paring knife. Open the pouch and let cool. Reduce the oven temperature to 350°F.

2. Add the hazelnuts to the baking sheet and cook for 8 to 10 minutes, until the skins start to split and flake off and they smell toasty. Transfer to a small bowl and cover with a folded dish towel. After about 10 minutes, unfold the towel and transfer the nuts to the towel; fold it over and rub vigorously to remove the skins. They won't all come off, and that's OK. Return them to one end of the baking sheet, and tip it at a 45-degree angle. The nuts will roll to one end, leaving the flaky skins behind. You can lift the nuts with a bench scraper to help the process along. Set aside a handful for the garnish.

3. Bring a medium saucepan of water to a boil and have a bowl of ice water standing by. Add the kale and boil just until wilted, 1 to 2 minutes, then use tongs to transfer the kale to the ice water. Drain and squeeze out all the water with your hands. You should have about ½ cup.

4. Combine the beet, garlic, kale, and the 3 tablespoons oil in a food processor and pulse until smooth with just a little texture, adding more oil if needed to loosen. Add the hazelnuts, cheese, ½ teaspoon salt, and red pepper flakes and pulse until the nuts are roughly chopped. Transfer to a bowl. (You'll have about 1 ¼ cups.)

5. Cook the pasta in well-salted water until al dente. Scoop up a cup of pasta water, then drain the pasta. Return the pasta to the pot and stir in about half of the pesto, adding enough pasta water to loosen (about ½ cup). Season with salt and pepper to taste and divide among four bowls. Roughly chop the reserved hazelnuts and sprinkle over top. Shave the radish (if using) over the pasta and serve with more cheese on the side.

You won't need all the pesto, but no worries: it will keep well in the refrigerator for several days, and you can swirl it into soup, top a ricotta-slathered piece of toast with it, or use it as a sandwich spread. You can also freeze it for up to 3 months for a future pasta dish.

Sub in walnuts or almonds if you don't want to bother toasting and peeling the hazelnuts.

VEG FORWARD

SERVES 4

MUSHROOM RISOTTO

Risotto isn't difficult to cook—it just requires some attention and care. You've got to use your instincts because there are so many variables: the size and shape of the pan (a low, wide saucepan is best), the type of stove you're using, and the heat level of the burner. The rice should always be thinly veiled in liquid and bubbling energetically; when the liquid's been absorbed, add some more. The exact amount isn't important. Contrary to lore, risotto does not need to be stirred constantly, just frequently. You can absolutely make a salad or set the table while you are cooking this. Stir more frequently and more vigorously in the second half of the cooking, when the grains begin to release their starch, which will help the rice become its creamiest. Although risotto is usually a one-pot affair, I think it's easiest to sauté the extra mushrooms in a separate skillet.

Ingredients

1 ounce dried porcini mushrooms

2 cups boiling water

2 tablespoons olive oil, divided

8 ounces cremini (Baby Bella) or shiitake mushrooms, trimmed and sliced

Kosher salt

3 1/2 cups chicken or vegetable stock (page 226)

2 tablespoons butter, divided

1 medium shallot, minced

1 1/2 cups Arborio rice

1/2 cup dry white wine

2 ounces grated Parmesan cheese, plus more for serving

Instructions

1. Put the dried mushrooms in a large measuring cup or deep medium bowl and pour the boiling water over them. Stir to make sure they are all moistened. Set aside to soak for 15 minutes.

2. Heat a large (12-inch) skillet over high heat. Add 1 tablespoon of the oil and the fresh mushrooms. Sprinkle lightly with salt and toss to coat evenly with the oil. Cook, stirring frequently, for 3 to 4 minutes, or until golden brown on the edges. Set aside off the heat.

3. Scoop the dried mushrooms out of the water, squeezing the excess liquid back into the bowl. Chop the mushrooms finely and set aside. Reserve the soaking liquid.

4. Put the stock and 1 1/2 cups of the reserved mushroom liquid (discard the rest) in a small saucepan on the back burner of the stove. Bring to a simmer, turn down to keep warm, and cover until ready to use. Have a soup ladle ready.

5. Heat a medium saucepan, preferably one more wide than deep, over medium heat. Add 1 tablespoon of the butter and the remaining tablespoon of oil. Add the shallot and cook for 2 to 3 minutes until translucent, turning down the heat if it threatens to brown.

6. Add the rice and the reserved dried mushrooms and cook for 2 to 3 minutes, stirring, until the grains look slightly translucent. Add the wine and cook until nearly absorbed, about 1 minute.

7. Add a ladleful of stock (it should be just enough to barely cover the surface of the rice). Cook at a lively simmer, stirring very frequently, until it's nearly absorbed, 2 to 3 minutes. Continue adding the stock in this way until the rice is very creamy, but still al dente, 15 to 20 minutes total. You may not need all of the liquid.

8. Rewarm the fresh mushrooms and stir half of them into the risotto. Stir in the remaining tablespoon butter and cheese and add salt and pepper to taste. Add more of the remaining liquid if needed to loosen the risotto (it should be a tiny bit soupy) and divide among four shallow bowls. Top with remaining mushrooms and serve immediately.

If you can find oyster, maitake, or chanterelle mushrooms, use them.

SERVES 4

RISOTTO CAKES

If you have leftover risotto, I've got you covered! Italians always have delicious ideas for leftovers, never wanting anything to go to waste. I hope you've already had the pleasure of eating a well-made Mushroom Risotto from the previous pages. With a few extra ingredients, these risotto cakes create a singular treat with a melted cheese center, designed to use up yesterday's risotto.

Ingredients

2 cups leftover risotto

1 large egg, beaten

¼ cup panko breadcrumbs

Fontina or mozzarella cheese, cut into 4 1-inch cubes

Olive oil or butter

Instructions

1. Heat the oven to 350°F.

2. Mix 2 cups cold leftover risotto, 1 large egg, beaten, and ¼ cup panko breadcrumbs in a medium bowl.

3. Add a pinch of red pepper flakes or Aleppo-style pepper and mix well.

4. Using dampened hands, scoop up about one quarter of the rice mixture. Press a cube of fontina or mozzarella cheese into the center of the rice, enclosing it all around, then flatten into a patty. Repeat, making 4 patties.

5. Use another ¼ cup panko to coat both sides of the patties.

6. Heat 1 tablespoon olive oil and 1 tablespoon butter in a large (12-inch) skillet over medium-high heat (or cook the patties in batches). Cook the patties for 4 to 5 minutes on the first side until golden brown. Flip the patties and cook for 1 minute and transfer the pan to the oven and cook for 10 minutes, until heated through. Serve hot.

VEG FORWARD

SERVES 4 TO 6

BUTTERNUT SQUASH GNOCCHI WITH BRUSSELS SPROUTS AND SAGE

Light-as-air potato gnocchi are laced with the sweetness of butternut squash. They're easier than you may think to make, and you'll look like a genius at your next dinner party. If the ratio of squash to potato is too high, the gnocchi will be gummy. So, if you need to add more flour to the dough, that's fine, but add as little as possible, so the texture stays light and airy.

For the gnocchi

1 large (about 10 ounces) russet potato, scrubbed and pricked with a fork

1 medium butternut squash (about 1 1/2 pounds), peeled, seeded, and cut into 1/2-inch cubes (about 4 cups)

1 teaspoon olive oil

Kosher salt and freshly ground pepper

1/2 cup grated Parmesan cheese

1 large egg

1 large egg yolk

Freshly grated nutmeg

Pinch of cayenne pepper

3/4 cup all-purpose flour, plus more as needed

For serving

2 tablespoons butter, plus more if needed

2 tablespoons olive oil, plus more if needed

8 to 10 sage leaves

2 cups Brussels sprouts, preferably small ones, trimmed and halved, or shredded if larger

Grated Parmesan cheese

Instructions

1. **To make the gnocchi:** Heat the oven to 400°F, with a rack in the middle. Place the potato directly on the middle rack. Toss the squash with oil, 1/2 teaspoon salt, and a few grinds of pepper. Spread in a single layer on a baking sheet and place on the same rack.

2. Bake the squash, stirring halfway through, until it's tender but not brown. Turn the potato and continue baking for 30 to 40 minutes longer until soft when squeezed. When the squash is cool, mash in a wide bowl with a large fork or potato masher.

3. When the potato is done, let it cool and peel off the skin. Add the potato to the bowl with the squash, and mash, using whatever you used to mash the squash. Mix until you no longer see any spots of potato.

4. The mixture should be cool by now, but if not, let it cool a bit more. Use the fork to incorporate the cheese, then make a well in the center. Add the eggs, 1/2 teaspoon salt, nutmeg, and cayenne. Beat with the fork, and gradually incorporate the squash mixture, continuing until it is thoroughly mixed, switching to a rubber spatula.

5. Sprinkle the flour over the top of the mixture and mix well. Briefly knead in the bowl with floured hands to form a smooth dough, and turn out on a lightly floured work surface. If the dough feels very sticky, add more flour, 1 tablespoon at a time, until it's no longer sticky.

6. Line a baking sheet with wax paper and flour the paper. Divide the dough into 4 pieces. Roll each piece into a rope about 3/4 inch in diameter. If it becomes too long to manage, cut the rope in half. Cut the rope into 1-inch pieces and transfer to the baking sheet. The gnocchi can be refrigerated for a few hours or frozen for up to 3 months (freeze the gnocchi on the baking sheet and then transfer them to a zip-top bag).

7. Bring a large pot of water to a boil and add a generous amount of salt. Add half the gnocchi. They will float to the top after about a minute but let them cook for 2 to 3 minutes longer. Use a slotted spoon to transfer them to a paper towel–lined plate. Remove the towel after a minute so they don't stick. Repeat with the remaining gnocchi.

8. **To serve:** Heat a large skillet over medium heat and add the butter and oil. Add half the boiled gnocchi and scatter half the sage leaves in between. Cook for about 2 minutes per side until deep golden brown. Repeat with the remaining gnocchi. Transfer to a plate as they finish.

9. Add the Brussels sprouts to the hot pan, adding more butter and oil if needed, and cook for 2 to 3 minutes until tender and golden. Serve the gnocchi with more Parmesan.

SERVES 4 TO 6

LEEK AND SQUASH FARROTTO

Like the starchy rice varieties used for risotto, pearled farro also releases its starch into broth when cooked in the same style: stirred frequently, with hot liquid added gradually. The result is both creamy and comforting. Butternut squash cubes get a head start cooking in the broth, adding to the creaminess.

Ingredients

5 cups chicken or vegetable stock (page 226)

8 ounces butternut squash, cut into $1/2$-inch cubes (about 2 cups)

2 teaspoons olive oil

2 teaspoons plus 1 tablespoon butter

2 large leeks, halved lengthwise, sliced into half-moons, and well washed (about 2 cups)

2 garlic cloves, minced

1 tablespoon finely chopped fresh rosemary leaves

Kosher salt and freshly ground pepper

$1 1/2$ cups pearled farro, rinsed

$1/2$ cup dry white wine

1 fluffy cup grated Parmesan cheese (1 ounce), plus more for serving

Instructions

1. Combine the stock and the squash in a small saucepan. Bring to a boil and simmer for 5 minutes until slightly softened. Keep warm over low heat, covered.

2. In a wide, shallow saucepan, heat the oil and 2 teaspoons butter over medium heat. Add the leeks, garlic, and rosemary, season with salt and pepper, and cook, stirring, for 5 to 6 minutes, until the leeks are wilted. Add the farro and cook for 2 to 3 minutes longer, stirring. Add the wine and cook until evaporated, about 1 minute.

3. Add a ladleful of the stock and some of the squash, so the farro is thinly veiled in liquid. Cook at a brisk simmer, stirring frequently with a wooden spoon, and adding another ladleful when the first is nearly absorbed. Continue in this way for 20 to 25 minutes, until the farro is al dente. Add a little more liquid as needed to loosen.

4. Season to taste with salt and pepper. Stir in the remaining tablespoon of butter and the cheese. Serve in warm shallow bowls with more cheese on the side.

If you want a little more heft and aren't a vegetarian, skip the olive oil and butter and render the fat from some bacon, frying it until crisp. Remove the bacon, leaving some or all of the fat in the pan. Sprinkle the finished dish with the crisp bacon.

Garnish with toasted pepitas and a drizzle of nutty pumpkin seed oil to amp up the earthy flavors.

VEG FORWARD

VEG FORWARD

SERVES 4 AS A MAIN OR MORE AS A SIDE

SHAVED CAULIFLOWER WITH CHICKPEAS, FREEKEH, AND GREEN TAHINI-YOGURT SAUCE

For years, I've been roasting cauliflower in florets, usually with a flat side down, but one day I thought, *Why not just slice it really thin if it's caramelization I'm after?* That turns out to be a superior way to cook it. The skinny slices get crisp and brown all over, especially at the edges. Adding chickpeas and freekeh (or another grain; see notes below) makes this a full vegetarian meal.

Ingredients

2 medium heads cauliflower, about 2 1/2 pounds

1 (15.5-ounce) can chickpeas, drained, rinsed, and patted dry

1 large shallot, sliced lengthwise

3 to 4 tablespoons olive oil, as needed

1 teaspoon kosher salt

Freshly ground pepper

1 teaspoon garlic powder

2 cups cooked cracked freekeh (from 2/3 cup raw)

1/2 cup Green Tahini-Yogurt "Everything Sauce" (page 220)

Instructions

1. Heat the oven to 450°F, with racks in the upper and lower positions. Line two baking sheets with foil.

2. Trim the large stem from the bottoms of the heads of cauliflower. With the heads sitting on the flat side, cut into 1/2-inch-thick slices.

3. Divide the cauliflower between the baking sheets. (Don't crowd the pan, or the cauliflower won't brown well.) Divide the chickpeas and the shallot between the pans. Drizzle with the olive oil, using more or less as needed. Sprinkle with the salt, pepper, and garlic powder. Use your hands to make sure everything is well coated and spread out evenly.

4. Place the baking sheets on the racks and roast for 15 minutes. Remove the pans one at a time to turn the cauliflower pieces. Reverse the positions of the pans from front to back and top to bottom and roast for another 10 to 15 minutes, or until everything is evenly golden brown.

5. Serve on top of freekeh with the Green Tahini-Yogurt Sauce on the side.

Feel free to use cooked bulgur, farro, quinoa, or even brown rice in place of the freekeh.

Cauliflower heads can vary in size, so use a scale if you can, and your judgment for sure. The most important thing is not to crowd the baking sheets.

Use as much oil as you need to coat the cauliflower.

I like to mix cauliflower colors if I can, orange and purple being my top picks.

If you have a convection option on your oven, use that and preheat it to 425°F. It will help the cauliflower brown and caramelize without steaming.

To cook the freekeh: Bring 1 1/3 cups water to a boil in a small saucepan. Add 2/3 cup freekeh and 1/4 teaspoon kosher salt and return to a boil. Turn down to a simmer, cover, and cook for 10 to 15 minutes, or until all the water is absorbed. Fluff with a fork.

VEG FORWARD

SERVES 4 GENEROUSLY

RED LENTIL AND VEGETABLE SOUP WITH CRISPY SPICED CHICKPEAS

This fragrantly spiced soup is worthy of a dinner party. It's positively brimming with cauliflower, squash, and carrots, and it's beautiful. The red lentils and the coconut milk make it thick and creamy, and the crispy chickpeas add substance. Serve the garnishes on the side and let guests customize their bowls.

For the soup

1 tablespoon olive oil

1 tablespoon butter

1 medium onion, chopped

2 large garlic cloves, minced

1 tablespoon minced serrano or jalapeño pepper

1 teaspoon turmeric

1 teaspoon ground coriander

1/8 teaspoon cayenne pepper

1 cup red lentils, rinsed

1 teaspoon kosher salt

Freshly ground pepper

4 cups chicken or vegetable stock (page 226), plus more if needed

1 can coconut milk, well stirred

1 pound kabocha squash (unpeeled) or butternut squash (peeled), seeded, and cut into 3/4-inch cubes (about 3 cups)

1/2 small head cauliflower (10 ounces), cut into small florets

1 cup thinly sliced carrots

For the crispy chickpeas

1 1/2 tablespoons vegetable oil

1 (15.5-ounce) can chickpeas, drained, rinsed, and patted dry

1/2 teaspoon ground coriander

1/4 teaspoon turmeric

1/2 teaspoon paprika

1/4 teaspoon kosher salt

Instructions

1. **To make the soup:** In a small Dutch oven or soup pot, heat the olive oil and butter over medium-low heat. Add the onion and cook, stirring occasionally, for about 4 minutes, until it starts to soften. Add the garlic and serrano or jalapeño and cook for 2 minutes. Add the spices and cook for 2 minutes, stirring.

2. Add the lentils, salt, a few generous grinds of black pepper, the stock, and the coconut milk and bring to a boil. Reduce the heat and simmer for 10 minutes, partially covered.

3. Add the squash, cauliflower, and the carrots and continue simmering, partially covered, until all the vegetables are tender, 20 to 25 minutes. Add more stock if soup is too thick.

4. **Meanwhile, make the crispy chickpeas:** Heat the oil in a large skillet. Toss the chickpeas with the spices, coating them well. Add them to the oil and cook, stirring, for about 8 minutes until crispy.

5. **To serve:** Ladle the soup into warm bowls and top with the chickpeas. Garnish with cilantro leaves, shredded mint, yogurt, chilies, lime wedges, and sriracha on the side.

If you want to make this soup quicker for a weeknight, just add the chickpeas directly to the soup instead of crisping them.

Stir in some baby spinach just before serving if you want more greens.

You can make the soup even more substantial by poaching fish fillets like fluke, flounder, or red snapper in the hot soup for 5 minutes before serving. The same can easily be done with shrimp or chicken; just make sure they're thoroughly cooked.

I sometimes add tofu to the leftover soup for a quick and satisfying lunch.

For serving, garnish with any of the following: cilantro leaves, shredded mint, yogurt, thinly sliced serrano or jalapeño chilies, lime wedges, or sriracha.

VEG FORWARD

VEG FORWARD

SERVES 6 TO 8

LENTIL AND BEET SALAD

I first made this salad for guests on a day when we had an outing right before lunch, and I not only needed something that I could make ahead but that would also get better as it sat. Simple boiled beets (they're the easiest to peel) contribute to the flavor and juiciness of the dressing, which is scented with orange and spiked with garlic and mustard. After the lentils have absorbed all this goodness for a day or two, crunchy arugula and creamy goat cheese are folded in just before serving. Topping the salad off with dramatic sliced watermelon radishes is my favorite party trick, but ordinary red radishes work too.

Ingredients

1 ½ cups small green (Puy) lentils, rinsed

4 cups water

1 ¾ teaspoons kosher salt, divided

2 large garlic cloves

1 bay leaf

3 medium beets, trimmed and scrubbed

2 tablespoons freshly squeezed orange juice

1 tablespoon balsamic vinegar

1 teaspoon Dijon mustard

Freshly ground pepper

4 tablespoons olive oil

2 cups baby arugula

½ cup thinly sliced shallots (1 small)

2 ounces goat cheese, crumbled

1 watermelon or red radish, very thinly sliced

Instructions

1. Add the lentils to a medium saucepan and add the water. Add 1 teaspoon of salt, the garlic, and the bay leaf and bring to a boil. Simmer over low heat for 10 to 12 minutes until almost tender. Turn off the heat and let sit for 5 minutes so they continue to gently cook. Drain, rinse, and set aside. Discard the bay leaf and reserve the garlic cloves.

2. Add the beets to the saucepan. Cover by 2 inches with water and add ½ teaspoon salt. Bring to a boil, reduce the heat, and cook at a lively simmer for about 30 minutes, or until a paring knife inserted into a beet meets no resistance. Turn off the heat and let the beets cool in the liquid for at least 10 minutes so they continue to gently cook. Drain and cover with cold water right in the pot. Slip the skins off under the water.

3. Meanwhile, in a small bowl, mash the reserved garlic cloves with a fork. Stir in the orange juice, vinegar, mustard, and the remaining ¼ teaspoon salt and pepper. Slowly mix in the oil.

4. Cut the beets in half lengthwise (or quarter if large) and slice them about ¼ inch thick. Mix with the dressing while they're still warm. Stir in the lentils and adjust the seasonings. At this point, you can refrigerate for up to 2 days or proceed with the recipe. Bring back to room temperature when ready to serve and adjust seasonings to taste.

5. When ready to serve, toss with the arugula and the shallots.

6. Gently fold in the cheese and transfer to a serving bowl. Use a mandoline or a sharp knife to thinly slice the radish and strew over the top.

Small black beluga lentils, so named because they resemble caviar, can be used too, but avoid the more common brown lentils, which won't stay firm enough for a salad when cooked.

VEG FORWARD

SERVES 4

POBLANO CORN CHOWDER

Toward the end of corn season when the weather first starts turning chilly, I make this chowder. Chowders are traditionally milk- or cream-based, but I build a richer flavor by using vegetable ingredients, with just a touch of dairy to finish. Pureeing a portion of the soup and stirring it back in makes it satisfyingly thick and creamy.

Ingredients

1 poblano pepper

1 tablespoon butter or olive oil

2 cups sliced, well-washed leeks (about 2), white and light green parts only

2 celery stalks, finely diced

1 tablespoon finely diced jalapeño or serrano pepper (or to taste)

1/2 teaspoon kosher salt

4 cups fresh corn kernels, cut from 3 to 4 ears

12 ounces baby Yukon Gold potatoes, halved or quartered

4 cups corn cob stock (page 226), chicken stock, or vegetable stock (page 226)

A few sprigs fresh thyme

1 bay leaf

1/4 to 1/2 cup milk or heavy cream (optional)

Oyster crackers for serving

Instructions

1. Roast the pepper directly on top of the burner of a gas stove or over a gas grill, turning as needed until blackened all over, 6 to 8 minutes total. Transfer to a plastic bag until cool enough to handle, about 15 minutes. Use the bag to help slide the skin from the peppers, then remove the pepper from the bag. Slice it open and remove the seeds, stem, and any remaining skin. Avoid rinsing the pepper so as not to wash away any of the flavor. Set aside.

2. Heat a medium Dutch oven or a large saucepan over medium heat. Add the butter or oil and add the leeks, celery, jalapeño, and 1/2 teaspoon of salt. Cook, stirring occasionally, until the vegetables are wilted and softened, 8 to 10 minutes.

3. Add the corn, potatoes, stock, thyme, and bay leaf and bring to a boil. Reduce to a simmer and cook, partially covered, for 15 to 20 minutes, or until the potatoes are tender enough for the tip of a paring knife to slide right in.

4. Add the milk or cream (if using) and heat gently until hot. Discard the thyme and bay leaf. Scoop 2 cups of the soup into a blender and puree until smooth. Return all but 1/2 cup of the puree to the soup. Add the poblano to the blender and puree again until smooth. Slowly add the poblano mixture back to the soup, tasting as you go, until the spice level is agreeable to you. Serve hot with oyster crackers.

VEG FORWARD

SERVES 4

ROASTED AND RAW BRUSSELS SPROUTS SALAD

If you like a good kale salad—who doesn't?—then you will love Brussels sprouts salad. There are lots of good things going on here: crunch and char and cheese and bacon. As with a kale salad, the raw shredded sprouts are best left to marinate for up to an hour, making it a perfect make-ahead dish. Later, the whole leaves, which are trimmed off, are briefly roasted, along with shallots and almonds. If possible, wait until the moment before serving to add the hot roasted ingredients so you can enjoy the contrast of the crispy leaves and hot almonds against the crunchy and tangy shredded sprouts. Using a food processor with the slicing blade shreds the sprouts in seconds; they are a bit small and fiddly to slice on a mandoline. The shredding can also be accomplished with a sharp knife.

Ingredients

1 pound (or two 9-ounce containers) large Brussels sprouts

2 tablespoons lemon juice

3/4 teaspoon kosher salt, divided

1 medium shallot, halved

2 tablespoons red wine vinegar

1 tablespoon Dijon mustard

1 tablespoon whole-grain mustard

1/2 teaspoon maple syrup or honey

Freshly ground pepper

5 tablespoons extra-virgin olive oil, divided

1 1/2 ounces aged Gouda

3 ounces thick-cut bacon or pancetta (optional)

1/3 cup whole raw almonds, roughly chopped

Instructions

1. Trim the sprouts, cutting a good 1/4 inch off the bottom. Pull off the large dark green leaves and the first layer of lighter green leaves. You should have about 4 cups. Set aside; you will roast these whole leaves later.

2. Shred the remaining sprouts thinly, using a food processor fitted with the slicing blade, or by hand with a knife. You should have about 4 cups. Toss the shredded sprouts with the lemon juice and 1/4 teaspoon of the salt, rubbing with your hands to help soften them. Set aside for about 1/2 hour.

3. Heat the oven to 400°F. Finely mince one quarter of the shallot and mix with the vinegar in a glass jar or other microwave-safe container. Heat for 30 seconds in the microwave. Add the mustards, honey, 1/4 teaspoon of the salt, and pepper. Slowly stream in 4 tablespoons of the oil and drizzle about half the dressing onto the shredded raw sprouts, mixing thoroughly. Grate half the cheese and toss that in too. Transfer to a serving bowl.

4. Cut the bacon or pancetta (if using) into 1/4-inch pieces and spread out on a baking sheet. Roast for about 8 minutes, until starting to brown and crisp. Thinly slice the rest of the shallot lengthwise and add to the baking sheet with the bacon, along with the almonds. Toss to coat and cook for 8 minutes until everything is starting to brown and crisp. Toss the reserved whole sprout leaves with the remaining tablespoon oil and sprinkle lightly with the remaining 1/4 teaspoon salt. Use your hands to coat the leaves thoroughly and add to the baking sheet, sprinkling them on top of the other ingredients. Roast, tossing once or twice until the sprouts start to crisp and brown, 12 to 14 minutes.

5. Add the roasted ingredients to the shredded leaves in the bowl and toss. Grind more pepper on top and shave the remaining cheese with a vegetable peeler on top. Serve with extra dressing on the side.

If you can't find aged Gouda, use Parmesan or extra-sharp Cheddar.

If you're skipping the bacon or pancetta, use a few teaspoons of olive oil at the beginning of step 4.

VEG FORWARD

SERVES 4

SKILLET-ROASTED BEETS WITH BUTTERED KASHA AND WALNUTS

The combination of ingredients in this restaurant-style "salad" evokes my Eastern European roots. Caramelized roasted beets are the headliner, propped up by a creamy yogurt mixture tinged with mustard and horseradish. A sprinkling of lightly crisped, butter-toasted cooked kasha and walnuts adds a pleasant chew and a distinct earthiness. There are a few moving parts to the recipe, but none of them are difficult, and they come together harmoniously on the plate. Other cooked grains like farro, freekeh, or bulgur can stand in for the kasha.

Ingredients

6 medium or 8 small beets (about 1 pound), plus 1 raw for slicing (optional)

1 tablespoon olive oil

Kosher salt and freshly ground pepper

1 cup Greek yogurt

2 teaspoons prepared horseradish

1 teaspoon country or regular Dijon mustard

2 teaspoons unsalted butter

1 1/2 cups cooked whole kasha (buckwheat groats), from 1/2 cup dry, cooled

1/3 cup walnuts

1 small cucumber, peeled and diced

A handful of chopped dill

Instructions

1. Heat the oven to 425°F, with a large (12-inch) cast-iron skillet in the oven. Trim the stems of the beets to about 1/2 inch. Scrub them and use a peeler to remove any hairy roots or other gnarly parts. Cut them in halves or quarters depending on their size. Set aside one small beet. Toss the other beets with oil, sprinkle evenly with salt and pepper, and carefully toss into the skillet (it's hot!). Turn the beets cut side down. Roast for 30 to 35 minutes, turning once, until a paring knife slides into the largest pieces with no resistance. Set aside.

2. Stir together the yogurt, horseradish, and mustard, 1/4 teaspoon salt, and pepper and set aside.

3. Melt the butter over medium-high heat in a medium skillet and add the cooked kasha and the walnuts. Cook, tossing, for 5 to 7 minutes until the grains are crispy and golden brown. Season with 1/2 teaspoon salt.

4. Spread some of the yogurt on each of four plates or on a large platter. Divide the cooked beets among the plates and sprinkle with the kasha mixture, cucumbers, and the dill. Thinly slice the reserved raw beet (if using) and arrange on top. Serve warm or at room temperature.

Many supermarkets have whole buckwheat groats, but you have to know where to look. They're almost always found in the kosher section with the matzo and jarred gefilte fish. (Wolff's kasha is a common brand.) Make sure to buy whole kasha for this recipe rather than medium or coarse grind.

To cook the kasha: Bring a scant cup of water to a boil in a small saucepan. Add the kasha and 1/4 teaspoon salt and bring to a boil. Turn down to a simmer, cover, and cook for 10 minutes. Transfer to a bowl or plate to cool.

VEG FORWARD

SERVES 4 TO 6

CHARRED EGGPLANT WITH TAHINI-YOGURT SAUCE

When eggplant is charred—and I mean deeply charred—over a direct flame (or failing that, under a broiler), the insides turn creamy and soft. This dish is kind of a deconstructed baba ghanoush, where the eggplant is left intact instead of being mashed or pureed, with the tahini sauce, fresh herbs, lemony sumac, and juicy pomegranate seeds mixing and mingling as you scoop it up with warm bread. Think of this as something to make in early fall, when eggplant is plentiful, but it's a great dish for late summer too, or anytime you find nice, firm, shiny eggplant in the market.

For the sauce

2 tablespoons tahini

1/2 cup Greek yogurt

1/2 teaspoon Big Batch Roasted Garlic (page 217) or 1 small garlic clove, grated on a Microplane

2 tablespoons lemon juice, plus more for drizzling

1/2 teaspoon kosher salt

Sriracha

Water, as needed, to thin

For the eggplant

4 small eggplant (about 1 1/2 pounds total)

Handful of mint leaves

Handful of Italian parsley leaves

Ground sumac (optional, but nice)

Harissa sauce (optional, but nice)

Flaky salt

1/3 cup pomegranate seeds (optional, but nice)

Warm pita or other flatbread for serving

Instructions

1. **To make the sauce:** Combine tahini, yogurt, and garlic in a small bowl, and mix with a fork until smooth. Add lemon juice, salt, and sriracha to taste. Thin as needed with water to the desired consistency. You want it thick but spreadable. Refrigerate for up to 3 days if not serving right away.

2. **To make the eggplant:** Heat a gas grill to high. Poke each eggplant a few times with the tip of a paring knife. Roast the eggplants, giving them a quarter turn every 4 to 5 minutes until well charred on all sides and the flesh is very soft and creamy, 20 to 25 minutes.

3. Remove from the grill and place in a bowl until cool enough to handle. Pour off any accumulated liquid. Peel the charred skin off, leaving the eggplant and the stem intact.

4. Spread the sauce on a small platter and arrange the eggplants on top. Sprinkle generously with mint, parsley, and sumac (if using) and drizzle with harissa (if using). Sprinkle with flaky salt and pomegranate seeds (if using) and serve with warm flatbreads.

Instead of grilling, you can char the eggplants right on the burner of your gas stove. If you don't have that, use your broiler. Before cooking the eggplants, poke them several times with the tip of a paring knife so they don't explode.

To cook the eggplant directly on a gas burner: Line the surface of the stovetop around the burners with foil to keep the stovetop clean. Turn the burner to its highest setting. Using metal tongs, put the eggplant directly in the flame, turning frequently, until the skin is completely blackened and the flesh is very soft, 5 to 10 minutes or longer.

To cook the eggplant under the broiler: Heat the broiler to high, with a rack 6 inches from the heat source. Place the eggplants on a foil-lined baking sheet. Broil, turning frequently, until skin is completely blackened and the flesh is very soft, 15 to 20 minutes.

VEG FORWARD

SERVES 6 TO 8

PORCINI BRAISED ONIONS

I make these onions every year for Thanksgiving as a kind of a condiment alongside the turkey. Porcini add a deep umami flavor and incredible aroma to the already tasty cipollini, which are particularly sweet and perfect for cooking whole. They're great with any roast and are excellent with leftovers too, chopped up on a turkey sandwich. I've learned the hard way to serve them myself after everyone is seated. When they're on the buffet table, my guests can't resist taking big spoonfuls and they disappear before everyone gets some.

Ingredients

1 1/2 pounds small onions, like cipollini or pearl onions, or small shallots

1 ounce (1 small bag) dry porcini mushrooms (about 3/4 cup)

2 teaspoons olive oil

1 tablespoon fresh thyme leaves

1/2 teaspoon kosher salt

Freshly ground pepper

Few sprigs fresh thyme

1/2 cup chicken stock

Instructions

1. Heat the oven to 425°F. If using cipollini or pearl onions, bring a large saucepan of water to a boil, drop in the onions, and let cook for a minute or two. Drain in a colander and rinse with cold water. Peel. Trim the root end slightly but leave it intact to hold the onions together as they cook. If using shallots, just peel them normally.

2. Put the porcini in a 1-cup liquid measuring cup and pour boiling water over them, filling the cup. Let sit until softened and cooled, about 20 minutes. Lift the mushrooms from the liquid, chop finely, and reserve the liquid.

3. Toss the onions with the oil, thyme leaves, salt, and pepper and place in a medium cast-iron skillet or similar-size baking dish. Toss the thyme sprigs in and roast for 30 minutes, shaking several times until the onions are browned in spots and starting to soften.

4. Remove from the oven and add the chopped porcini and the chicken stock. Carefully pour in the porcini liquid (there should be about 1/2 cup), leaving any sand and grit behind in the cup. Bring to a simmer on the stovetop if using a skillet or cast-iron baking dish. (If using a ceramic baking dish, don't heat on the stovetop, but add 5 to 10 minutes to the cooking time, then return to the oven.) Bake for 20 to 30 minutes, stirring once or twice, until most of the liquid has been absorbed and onions are very soft. Serve warm.

You can use 1 1/2 pounds of small shallots instead of onions.

Look for peeled cipollini onions in your supermarket. They make this recipe a breeze.

VEG FORWARD

SERVES 4

RAINBOW CARROTS WITH BUCKWHEAT DUKKAH

Beautiful rainbow carrots nestle into a creamy yogurt base with a sprinkling of dukkah, a versatile topping of Egyptian origin made of toasted seeds, whole spices, and nuts. This one has the unorthodox addition of kasha, which gives it an irresistible nutty crunch.

For the carrots

18 to 20 thin rainbow carrots (2 to 3 bunches)

1 tablespoon olive oil

1 tablespoon honey

Kosher salt and freshly ground pepper

Grated zest and juice of 1 orange

3/4 cup labneh or thick Greek yogurt

1 tablespoon snipped chives

For the dukkah

2 tablespoons coriander seeds

1 tablespoon cumin seeds

2 tablespoons white sesame seeds

2 tablespoons black sesame seeds

1 tablespoon olive oil

1/2 cup whole kasha (buckwheat groats)

1/2 cup raw shelled pistachios

3/4 teaspoon flaky sea salt

Freshly ground pepper

Instructions

1. **To make the carrots:** Heat the oven to 425°F. Peel the carrots, leaving an inch or two of the stems on, if desired. Combine the oil and the honey in a small bowl, blending them with a fork. Spread the carrots on a baking sheet, toss with the oil mixture, and season with salt and pepper.

2. Roast until deeply browned in spots, shaking the pan occasionally, about 30 minutes. Turn the carrots, add the orange zest and juice, and cook for 10 to 15 minutes longer, until the liquid has mostly evaporated.

3. **Meanwhile, make the dukkah:** Heat a small skillet over medium heat. Add the coriander and cumin seeds and toast, shaking the pan until they're fragrant and have turned a shade darker, about 3 minutes. Transfer to a small bowl. Add the sesame seeds to the pan and cook until the white sesame is lightly toasted (you won't notice any change in the black sesame), about 2 minutes. Transfer to the same bowl.

4. Add the oil to the pan and add the kasha. Toast, stirring frequently, until golden brown, 4 to 6 minutes. Leave in the pan but remove from the heat.

5. Transfer the seeds in the bowl to a food processor and process until coarsely ground. Add the pistachios and pulse to chop coarsely. Return the ground seeds and nuts to the bowl and add the kasha. Season with salt and pepper. Stir to combine.

6. Spread the labneh or yogurt on the bottom of a large serving platter. Arrange the carrots on top, along with any juices from the pan. Sprinkle liberally with the dukkah. You can store the extra dukkah in a glass jar for a month or more. Top with the chives and serve.

The dukkah recipe will make more than you'll need for the carrots, but keep it on hand to sprinkle on yogurt or make a crust for fish or tofu. You can also sprinkle it in salads or use as a topping for hummus.

Rainbow carrots look striking, but any kind of fresh sweet carrot will work well. I usually seek out ones that still have their tops, rather than bagged carrots, when they will be the main ingredient for their good looks—and often better taste.

VEG FORWARD

163

SERVES 4 TO 6

ROASTED HONEYNUT SQUASH WITH QUINOA CRUNCH

Petite and sweet honeynut squash is a fairly new variety that grows in popularity and availability each year. The flesh is soft and creamy, and the skin is so thin that it's completely edible. You will most likely find this in your farmers' market at the height of the fall season, but any type of winter squash can be used here, butternut being the best substitution.

Ingredients

3 honeynut squash, split in half lengthwise and seeded

1 tablespoon olive oil

Kosher salt and freshly ground pepper

1 tablespoon butter, cut into slivers

2 tablespoons vegetable oil

½ cup cooked quinoa, preferably tricolor

¼ cup pepitas or sunflower seeds or a mix

¾ cup labneh or Greek yogurt

¼ cup lightly packed mint leaves, cut into thin strips

Sriracha or harissa to taste

Flaky sea salt for serving

Instructions

1. Heat the oven to 425°F. Place the squash cut side up on a foil-lined baking sheet. Drizzle with olive oil and season with salt and pepper to taste. Coat evenly using your hands. Turn the squash so the cut sides are down. Slide a bit of butter under each one. Bake for 20 to 25 minutes, until golden brown on the edges and tender.

2. Heat a medium skillet over medium-high heat and add the oil. When it's hot enough to make a little bit of quinoa sizzle, add the quinoa and cook for 1 to 2 minutes, until crispy. Add the seeds and cook for another 2 minutes until they are turning golden. Transfer to a paper towel–lined plate to cool, and sprinkle lightly with salt.

3. Spoon about 2 tablespoons of the labneh or yogurt into the cavity of each squash and sprinkle with the quinoa mixture and the mint. Drizzle with sriracha or harissa to taste and sprinkle with flaky sea salt. Serve hot or at room temperature.

Regular butternut squash, delicata, dumpling, or even acorn squash will all work well. If you're using a large butternut, cut in half, scoop out the seeds, and roast the same way until caramelized and soft (it will take a bit longer than the time given above), or cut into large chunks and turn once or twice while cooking.

VEG FORWARD

CUTTING WINTER SQUASH WITHOUT FEAR

Honeynut are softer than many varieties of other winter squash and can be easily cut in half with a sharp knife. But if you have a big tough-skinned squash and are daunted by the idea of cutting it in half, poke some holes in it with a fork or a metal skewer and microwave it whole for 3 to 5 minutes. This will soften the squash somewhat and make it easier to cut. Either way, gently rock the blade of your knife into the squash before applying any pressure. If the squash doesn't cleave cleanly into two equal halves, it's OK.

SERVES 6 TO 8

CARAMEL APPLE BROWN BUTTER BUCKLE

This cake practically buckles under the weight of all its silky apples and caramel, hence the name. It's a simple cake you can make after a trip to the apple orchard, and not too sweet. Enjoy it for breakfast or as a homey dessert with a little ice cream. Although it's best served warm, if you leave it out on your counter, you'll probably find that it disappears quickly, since people can't seem to resist "evening out the slices."

For the apples

2 tablespoons/28 g unsalted butter

$1/2$ cup/101 g granulated sugar

$2 1/2$ pounds Honeycrisp apples (about 3 large) peeled, cored, and cut into $1/2$-inch slices

1 teaspoon ground cinnamon

Big pinch of salt

For the cake

$1/2$ cup/113 g (1 stick) unsalted butter, cut up

$3/4$ cup/151 g granulated sugar

$1 1/4$ cups/160 g all-purpose flour

1 teaspoon baking powder

$1/2$ teaspoon kosher salt

$1/4$ teaspoon ground cardamom

2 large eggs

$1/2$ cup/123 g sour cream

1 teaspoon vanilla extract

1 tablespoon coarse sugar, such as Sugar in the Raw

Instructions

1. **To make the apples:** Heat the oven to 375°F. Heat a 9- or 10-inch cast-iron skillet over medium-high heat. Add the butter and let it melt. Add the sugar and stir to moisten. Heat until the sugar melts completely and starts to caramelize, stirring occasionally. Continue cooking until it's smooth and a deep amber color, about 5 minutes total. Carefully (don't splash!) add the apples all at once, along with the cinnamon and salt, and cook, stirring occasionally, until the apples become translucent and silky and the liquid has thickened, about 10 minutes. Slide the apple mixture onto a dinner plate and set aside. Rinse the skillet and return it to the stove.

2. **To make the cake:** Heat the skillet over medium heat and add the butter. Swirl the pan frequently until the butter turns nut brown and smells toasty, 2 to 5 minutes. (Even in a dark pan, you'll see the color turn, especially in the center when you swirl it.) Immediately transfer the butter to a medium bowl and set aside to cool slightly. Don't wash the skillet.

3. Combine the sugar, flour, baking powder, salt, and cardamom in a large bowl. Whisk to combine thoroughly.

4. Add the eggs, sour cream, and vanilla to the bowl with the butter and whisk to combine thoroughly. Fold the wet mixture into the dry using a rubber spatula, then fold in about half the apples, avoiding the extra caramel pooled on the plate. Transfer the batter to the buttered skillet and top with the remaining apples and the extra caramel. Sprinkle the raw sugar over top and bake for 40 to 50 minutes until a toothpick inserted in the center comes out clean and the cake is deep golden brown on the edges. Let cool for 10 minutes and serve warm.

You can use other apples, but make sure they are a variety that can stand up to the cooking process and not fall apart. Pink Lady, Cameo, Fuji, and Granny Smith are all good options, but use more apples as needed to approximate the weight given above. If the apples are small, you might need as many as six.

You can use any 9- or 10-inch skillet to cook the apples and make the brown butter, and then bake the buckle in a 9- or 10-inch cake pan. Just make sure to butter it first.

If baking in a shallow cake pan, put a baking sheet underneath to catch any errant juices.

You can use other dairy, like yogurt or labneh or crème fraiche, in place of the sour cream, but go for full-fat versions so the cake is tender.

VEG FORWARD

167

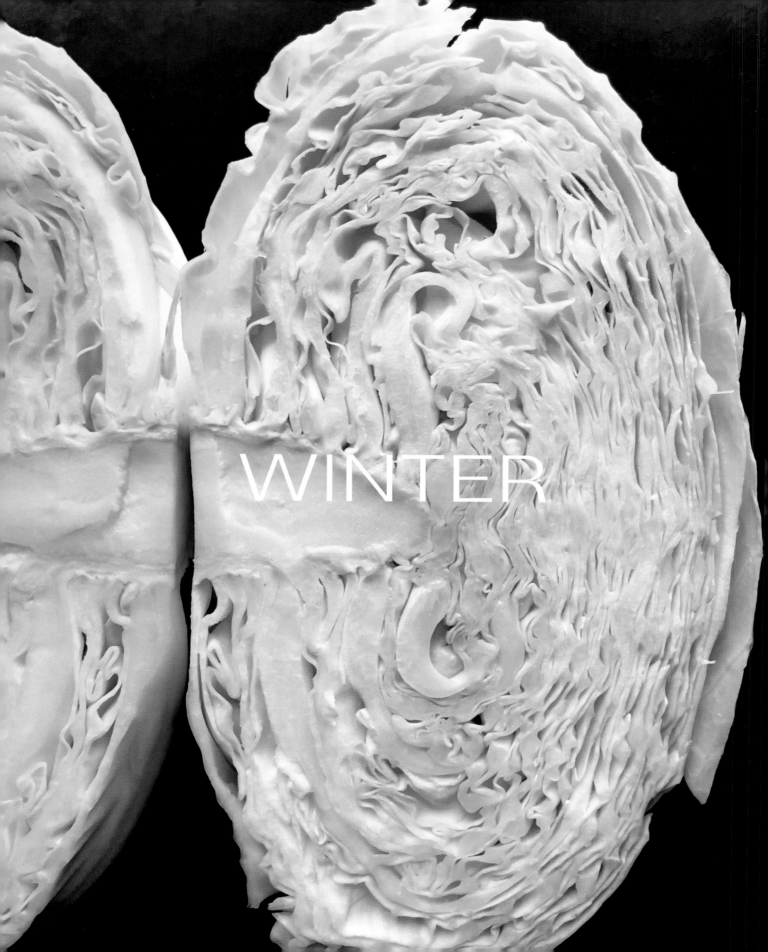

WINTER

VEG FORWARD

MAKES 8 CUPS

VEGGIE RAGÙ BOLOGNESE

This vegetarian version of the meat-based sauce from Bologna hews closely to the original in terms of technique. First, a soffritto of onion, celery, carrot, and fennel is cooked until nice and soft. Then, lots of chopped cauliflower and mushrooms (and even eggplant if you want) are added and it's all simmered with white wine and milk, which adds a silky creaminess to the sauce. Tomato paste is added, which deepens the flavors and brings everything together. Let the sauce bubble on the stove while you're doing other things. While the flavors will meld in as little as an hour, the sauce will be greatly improved if you cook it for the full 2 ½ hours.

Ingredients

1 ounce dried porcini mushrooms

2 tablespoons olive oil

1 large onion, finely diced

Kosher salt and freshly ground pepper

2 celery stalks, cut into ¼-inch dice

2 large or 4 small carrots, cut into ¼-inch dice

½ large or 1 small fennel bulb, cut into ¼-inch dice

4 garlic cloves, minced

1 (6-ounce) can tomato paste or a 7-ounce jar

1 cup dry white wine

2 portobello mushrooms (about 8 ounces) or 8 ounces cremini (Baby Bella) mushrooms, cut into ¼-inch dice

1 small head cauliflower (about 1 pound) or 1 (1-pound) eggplant, trimmed and chopped into ¼- to ½-inch pieces

1 ½ cups vegetable stock (page 226) or water

1 ½ cups whole milk

1 bay leaf

2 tablespoons porcini powder (optional)

Red pepper flakes

1 Parmesan rind (optional)

Instructions

1. Place the porcini in a small bowl or spouted measuring cup and pour 1 cup of boiling water over them. Stir to make sure they're all moistened and let them sit for about 15 minutes. Scoop the mushrooms out of the liquid, squeeze out the extra liquid, and reserve the liquid. Chop the mushrooms finely and set aside.

2. Meanwhile, heat a large Dutch oven over medium heat. Add the oil and the onion and season with 1 teaspoon salt. Cook for 5 to 6 minutes, until starting to turn translucent. Add the celery, carrots, and fennel, season with another ½ teaspoon salt and pepper, and cook until softened, about 15 minutes. Raise or lower the heat as needed so the vegetables are cooking at a good clip, but not browning. (The exact timing will depend on your pot and your stove.) Add the garlic and the soaked porcini mushrooms and cook for 10 minutes longer, stirring often.

3. At this point you might want to raise the heat a little; this is an important step in developing flavor. Clear a spot on the bottom of the pot so you can brown the tomato paste directly and add the tomato paste. Cook for 5 to 10 minutes, stirring to slowly incorporate the vegetables into it and cooking until lightly burnished in color and beginning to stick to the bottom of the pot.

4. Add the wine and cook, stirring, until evaporated, about 1 minute. Add the mushrooms and cauliflower or eggplant, season with ¼ teaspoon salt, and cook, covered, stirring once or twice, for about 10 minutes, until the veggies start to wilt.

5. Add the reserved porcini liquid, stock or water, milk, bay leaf, porcini powder (if using), red pepper flakes, and Parmesan rind (if using) and stir well. Add a little more salt to taste and plenty of pepper. Cover and cook over the lowest heat possible so the sauce is faintly bubbling and cook for at least 1 hour and as long as 2 ½ hours, stirring occasionally.

6. Serve with any pasta shape, passing red pepper flakes, black pepper, and Parmesan at the table. Or use to make the lasagna on page 175. The sauce keeps well in the refrigerator for 2 or 3 days, or it can be frozen for a month or two (or even longer).

You can definitely play around with which vegetables you use. You can either swap the eggplant for the cauliflower or use both for more flavor and a bigger yield, which is not a bad idea if your goal is to make the lasagna on page 175.

To serve the sauce with pasta, heat 3 cups of the sauce in a large skillet. Add 1 pound cooked pasta and cook until heated through, adding some pasta water if needed.

SERVES 4

FUSILLI WITH SOFT-COOKED BROCCOLI AND OLIVES

You don't want crisp, bright green florets here. The idea is to cook the broccoli down fairly quickly until it is soft and falling apart but still retains some freshness and bright color. Buttery oil-cured black olives add nuggets of interest to the sauce, which can be put together in the time it takes to boil the pasta. This is a great budget meal.

Ingredients

Kosher salt and freshly ground pepper

2 large broccoli crowns (about 1 1/4 pounds), trimmed

1/2 pound fusilli, preferably fusilli corti bucati

2 tablespoons olive oil

4 large garlic cloves (or more to taste), minced

6 anchovy fillets, rinsed and chopped

1/4 to 1/2 teaspoon red pepper flakes, to taste

16 oil-cured black olives, pitted and very roughly chopped (about 1/3 cup)

1 tablespoon unsalted butter

Grated pecorino or Parmesan for serving

Instructions

1. Bring a large pot of salted water to a boil. Cut the broccoli crowns into large chunks. Drop the broccoli into the boiling water and cook for 5 minutes, until tender. A paring knife should slide right into the stem with no resistance. Scoop the broccoli out with tongs or a strainer; keep the water boiling. Rinse the broccoli in a colander with cold water. Drain on paper towels, gently squeezing out excess water. Chop the broccoli into small pieces.

2. Add the pasta to the pot.

3. Meanwhile, heat the oil in a large (12-inch) skillet over medium heat. Add the garlic, anchovies, and red pepper flakes. Cook, stirring and mashing the anchovies with the back of a wooden spoon, for 3 to 4 minutes until the garlic is golden. Raise heat to medium-high. Add the broccoli and a ladleful (about 1 cup) of pasta water to the pan, and cook, stirring for about 5 minutes, adding more water as needed to achieve a cohesive sauce. Add the olives and add salt and pepper to taste.

4. Scoop some more pasta water from the pot. Drain the pasta and add to the pan and stir to coat, again adding more pasta water as needed to help the sauce coat the pasta evenly. Add the butter and stir until melted.

5. Divide among four bowls and serve with grated cheese and red pepper flakes on the side.

SERVES 8 TO 10

VEGGIE BOLOGNESE LASAGNA

This one's a project, to be sure, but an enjoyable one with loads of payoff. Even devoted carnivores will be satisfied with the "meatiness" of this dish, and at the end, you'll have a meal that feeds a crowd with absolutely no last-minute prep. There are a couple of directions you can go with the pasta portion of this recipe. The most time-consuming one, but definitely the most delicious, is to make the fresh pasta sheets yourself, cooking them and layering them assembly-line style, as described below. The next option is to use no-boil lasagna noodles, which is obviously easiest, since all you need to do is make the sauces and layer the dish. You could also use dried lasagna noodles, but this is my last choice, since it takes up a lot of space and it's hard to handle the slippery noodles. Whichever method and pasta you choose, the finished dish is so satisfying and craveable.

Ingredients

Soft butter for the dish

Béchamel Sauce (page 219), warmed if cold from the fridge

Veggie Ragù Bolognese (page 171)

8 uncooked fresh pasta sheets (page 208), or 15 sheets (1 box) no-boil lasagna noodles

1 cup/2 ounces grated Parmesan cheese

2 cups/8 ounces fontina cheese, chopped into small pieces

Instructions

1. Heat the oven to 375°F. Butter a 3-quart oval or 9-by-13-inch baking dish.

2. **If using fresh pasta:** Set yourself up assembly-line style to save space. Put a wide pot of salted water on to boil. Set a bowl of ice water next to the stove, with a baking sheet lined with an absorbent kitchen towel next to that. Set out your baking dish, sauces, and cheeses.

3. Slip 2 sheets of dough into the boiling water and boil for about 1 minute. Carefully fish them out (I like to use a spider/strainer and a wooden spoon to grab them) and spread them out flat on the towel-lined pan. Blot the tops with another towel.

4. Spread the dish with a scant $1/2$ cup of the béchamel, using the back of a spoon or small offset spatula to spread evenly. Cover with the 2 sheets of pasta, letting them overlap and come up the sides. Trim if needed. Follow with 1 $1/2$ cups of the Bolognese sauce and a scant $3/4$ cup of the béchamel. Sprinkle with $1/4$ cup of the Parmesan and a quarter of the fontina.

5. Repeat the process, cooking the pasta and topping with the sauces and cheese until you have 4 layers, ending with the sauces and cheeses on top. If you are using no-boil lasagna, simply layer the pasta with the sauces and cheeses. The assembled lasagna can be refrigerated for 2 days or frozen for a few months before baking.

6. Cover tightly with buttered foil, place the baking dish on a baking sheet, and bake for 40 minutes, or until hot in the center. Remove the foil and continue baking for 20 more minutes until bubbling and golden brown on top.

7. Let cool for about 30 minutes before cutting and serving.

If using no-boil lasagna sheets, use 4 sheets on each of the first 3 layers, and the final 3 for the top.

If freezing, defrost for 2 days in the refrigerator before baking. Let come to room temperature for 2 hours. Bake for 1 $1/2$ hours covered, and 20 minutes uncovered.

VEG FORWARD

SERVES 4 TO 6

MUSHROOM BOURGUIGNON

I've made a lot of beef Bourguignon in my life, including more times than I can remember on the set of *Julie & Julia*. It's the perfect thing to serve on a cold winter night for a cozy dinner party, but I've realized that what I love most about the dish isn't the meat but the sauce and vegetables. Normally, a stew is built on a *fond*, the caramelized layer of flavor created when meat is seared. Here, onions and mushrooms—especially maitakes, which have a deep umami flavor and a meaty texture—create a robust foundation.

Ingredients

1 ounce dried porcini mushrooms

2 cups boiling water

2 to 3 tablespoons olive oil, divided

1 tablespoon butter

1 pound cremini or white mushrooms, trimmed and quartered (halved if small)

8 ounces pearl onions, peeled

Kosher salt and freshly ground pepper

1/2 pound maitake mushrooms, bottom trimmed, clusters pulled apart into pieces

1 large shallot, minced (about 1/2 cup)

2 to 3 garlic cloves, minced

1 tablespoon chopped fresh rosemary

1 tablespoon tomato paste

2 tablespoons all-purpose flour

1 cup dry red wine

1 cup vegetable stock (page 226) or chicken stock

1 bunch thin carrots (about 10 ounces) cut into 2 1/2-inch lengths, halved lengthwise if thick

Sprig of thyme

Oven-Baked Polenta (page 208), mashed potatoes, or cooked egg noodles

Chopped Italian parsley

Instructions

1. Place porcini mushrooms in a 2-cup liquid measuring cup or container and pour the boiling water over them. Set aside to soften, pushing the mushrooms under the liquid now and then.

2. Heat a large (12-inch) skillet over medium-high heat. Add 1 tablespoon of the olive oil (or 2 tablespoons if using all creminis) and the butter. Add the cremini mushrooms and the onions and season with salt and pepper. Cook, tossing frequently, for about 10 minutes. The mushrooms will exude liquid, then caramelize, and the onions will brown in spots. Transfer to a plate. If using maitake, add another tablespoon of oil to the pan and repeat the process, transferring to the plate. Let the pan cool down a bit (it will be hot).

3. Scoop the porcini mushrooms out of the liquid and squeeze the excess liquid back into the cup. Finely chop the mushrooms and reserve the liquid.

4. Set the skillet over medium-low heat and add the remaining 1 tablespoon oil. Add the shallot, garlic, 1/2 teaspoon salt, rosemary, and chopped porcini mushrooms. Cook, stirring frequently, for 8 to 10 minutes, or until the shallots and garlic have softened.

5. Add the tomato paste and cook for 1 minute until lightly brown. Add the flour and cook for 1 minute longer, stirring.

6. Add the wine, raise the heat to medium, and use a wooden spoon to scrape up the brown bits on the bottom of the pan. Cook until evaporated, 1 to 2 minutes. Add the stock and the reserved porcini liquid, pouring it off carefully, leaving any grit at the bottom. Transfer the mixture to a small Dutch oven.

7. Add the carrots, thyme sprig, and the reserved mushrooms and pearl onions to the pot and cook, partially covered, for 1 hour and 15 minutes, until the carrots and pearl onions are tender. Stir occasionally while the stew is cooking. If, in the last 30 minutes of cooking, it looks too thin, remove the lid to let it thicken.

8. Adjust the seasonings, discard the thyme sprig, and serve over baked polenta, mashed potatoes, or egg noodles, with parsley sprinkled on top.

VEG FORWARD

TO PEEL PEARL ONIONS
To peel pearl onions more easily, add them to a saucepan of boiling water. Let sit until cool enough to handle. Trim off the hairy root, being careful not to cut too far into the onion so they stay together, and peel off the skin. If this sounds like too much work for you, look for the ones that come already peeled.

SERVES 4 TO 6

SMASHED POTATO AND SHALLOT GRATIN

The idea for this dish literally came to me in a dream. What if I smashed whole roasted potatoes right in the baking dish, then poured roasted garlic-laced cream over them, and baked them with a scattering of Parmesan until they were crispy and golden and delicious? The result is a recipe you'll want to keep handy. The use of cream is judicious, and most of it is absorbed by the potatoes, resulting in a rich but not overly heavy gratin. The shallots end up caramelized and sticky and you'll find yourself digging for them.

Ingredients

1 whole garlic head

2 tablespoons olive oil, plus more for drizzling

2 pounds baby potatoes, left whole

1 teaspoon kosher salt, divided

Freshly ground pepper

5 large or 8 small shallots, peeled and quartered lengthwise (about 2 cups)

15 to 20 sage leaves

1 cup (1/2 pint) light or heavy cream

1/2 cup finely grated Parmesan cheese

Instructions

1. Heat the oven to 425°F. Place the garlic on a square of aluminum foil and drizzle with some olive oil. Loosely but securely wrap and place directly on oven rack, seam side up. Bake for 1 hour until golden brown and very soft. Meanwhile, toss the potatoes with 1 tablespoon of the oil, 1/2 teaspoon of the salt, and pepper to taste in a large (3-quart) baking dish. Roll the potatoes around in the dish to coat them well.

2. After the garlic has roasted for 20 minutes, put the potatoes in the oven and roast, shaking from time to time. Toss the shallots with the remaining 1 tablespoon olive oil and the sage leaves.

3. After the potatoes have roasted for 15 minutes, add the shallot mixture, distributing evenly over the potatoes and shaking the pan to mix it in. Return the pan to the oven and roast for 15 minutes longer.

4. Remove the pan from the oven and use a potato masher or sturdy mug to flatten each potato. By now, the garlic should be ready. Cut the very top off the garlic head (just enough to expose the cloves) using a steak knife or other serrated knife and squeeze the contents into a small bowl. Combine with the cream and stir with a fork, mashing the garlic and combining well. Add the remaining 1/2 teaspoon salt and pepper to taste. Pour over the potatoes, sprinkle with Parmesan, and return to the oven Bake for 20 to 25 minutes longer, until the top is deep golden brown. Serve.

VEG FORWARD

THE RIGHT DISH

I use an enameled cast-iron baking dish for many different things, from roasting a chicken to baking pasta dishes to making fruit crisps. It's the perfect vessel for this recipe too. Failing that, a ceramic baking dish works too, as does a large iron skillet. All the potatoes should fit easily in one layer, with a little room for the shallots.

To see if the dish is right, just tumble in the potatoes (before oiling them) and see if they fit in one layer.

SERVES 6 TO 8

ONION AND CABBAGE PANADE

Panade is a French cooking term that, loosely translated, means "bread thing." Classically it's a mixture of bread, milk, and seasonings that you use to keep things like meatloaf and meatballs moist and flavorful. This kind of panade is a little different. Think of the best part of French onion soup, but without much soup. The bread soaks it all up, so what you get is kind of a soupy bread pudding with plenty of cabbage and onions and a crusty, cheesy top. It's rustic comfort food at its best.

Ingredients

4 large Spanish onions (2 to 3 pounds)

1 tablespoon olive oil

2 tablespoons unsalted butter, divided

Kosher salt

About 1 cup water, as needed

$1/4$ cup Madeira, dry sherry, or cognac (optional)

Freshly ground pepper

$1/2$ large head green cabbage (about 1 pound), shredded

3 to 4 sprigs thyme

1 sourdough boule, sliced $1/2$ inch thick

4 cups vegetable stock (page 226) or beef or chicken stock, or more as needed

6 ounces Gruyère and/or fontina cheese, grated (about 2 cups)

2 ounces Parmesan cheese, grated (about 1 cup)

Instructions

1. Slice the onions in half lengthwise (from root to stem end), peel them, and slice about $1/4$ inch thick lengthwise (in the same direction).

2. Heat a large pot, braiser, or a shallow Dutch oven over medium-high heat and add the oil and 1 tablespoon of the butter. Add the onions and $1/2$ teaspoon salt and toss gently using tongs. If the onions are steaming and not browning after the first 5 minutes, turn the heat up to high. Cook for 12 to 14 minutes, stirring only occasionally so the onions have a chance to brown, by which time they should be soft and wilted, and starting to turn brown all over.

3. Add $1/4$ cup water and the Madeira, sherry, or cognac (if using; if not, increase the water to $1/2$ cup) and use a wooden spoon to scrape the bottom of the pan. Reduce the heat to low and cook for 25 to 30 minutes, stirring occasionally. Add more water, $1/4$ cup at a time, if the onions start to stick. Season with pepper to taste.

4. Add the cabbage (and a few tablespoons of water if needed), raise the heat to medium, and add $1/2$ teaspoon salt, the thyme, and more pepper. Cook, tossing occasionally, until wilted, then cover and continue cooking for 15 minutes, tossing occasionally, until soft. Uncover and reduce the heat to medium-low. Cook for 25 to 30 minutes, stirring occasionally and adding $1/4$ cup water if needed to prevent sticking, until very soft and brown. Remove the thyme stems and adjust the seasonings. Transfer to a bowl.

5. Add $1/2$ cup of water to deglaze the pot, scraping up any brown bits. Pour over the onions in the bowl and rinse the pot.

6. Heat the oven to 325°F. Melt 1 tablespoon of the butter in the same pot and then remove from the heat. Spread out half of the onion mixture on the bottom of the pot, followed by a layer of bread slices, tearing them to fit and create an even layer. Follow with the remainder of the onion mixture. Top with the remaining bread slices. You may not need all the bread; just use enough to fit.

7. Add 3 cups of the stock, or until you see it welling up to the same level as the top of the bread. Press down lightly with a spatula to help the bread absorb the liquid. Let sit for 10 minutes, then add the remaining cup of stock (or more as needed) to maintain the same level. Bring to a simmer on the stovetop and cover tightly with foil or with the lid of the pot. Place on a parchment- or foil-lined baking sheet and bake for 30 minutes, until steaming hot throughout. Remove the foil and top with the cheeses and cook for 30 to 40 minutes longer until the cheese has browned and the liquid is mostly absorbed. Serve hot in bowls.

VEG FORWARD

SERVES 4

ROASTED VEGETABLE HASH WITH HARISSA AND POACHED EGGS

This is the home you've been seeking for all your random root vegetables. You can use any mix—you don't have to stick to the ones listed here (see suggestions below). The vegetables get caramelized and concentrated, taking on a bit of each other's character. The beets especially stain everything a rosy color, like a traditional red flannel hash. The harissa adds some spicy kick, and the sugar in the ketchup helps with the caramelization process. You can serve the hash as suggested, with a runny poached egg on top, for brunch or dinner, or leave the eggs off and serve it as a side dish.

For the hash

1 large (about 1 pound) fennel bulb, trimmed and diced

2 medium beets, peeled and diced

1 watermelon radish or 2 to 3 regular radishes

1/2 large celeriac, peeled and trimmed, diced

1 sweet potato, diced

2 large parsnips, peeled and diced

1/2 large red onion, peeled and diced

3 tablespoons olive oil

1 teaspoon kosher salt

Freshly ground pepper

1 tablespoon chopped fresh rosemary

2 tablespoons ketchup

1 to 2 tablespoons harissa sauce, plus more for serving

1/4 cup chopped Italian parsley

For the eggs

4 large eggs

1/2 teaspoon kosher salt

1 tablespoon white vinegar

Instructions

1. **To make the hash:** Heat the oven to 450°F, with a rack in the middle. Line a baking sheet with foil and add the fennel, beets, radish, celeriac, sweet potato, parsnips, and onion. Drizzle with the oil and season with salt and pepper. Add the rosemary, ketchup, and harissa and toss together with your hands until everything is well coated.

2. Spread out into a single layer and roast for 30 minutes, then stir and toss. Roast for an additional 15 to 20 minutes until softened and turning golden. Taste the vegetables and stir in more harissa if needed, along with the parsley.

3. **Meanwhile, poach the eggs:** Bring 3 to 4 inches of water to boil in a wide saucepan. Place the eggs (still in their shells) in a bowl of hot water for 1 minute to warm them. Add the salt and vinegar to the saucepan, turn off the heat, and add eggs, one at a time, by cracking each into a small bowl and slipping it into the water. Return the pan to low heat so the water is barely simmering. Gently loosen the eggs from the bottom of the pan with a slotted spoon after 2 minutes. Remove them with the spoon after a total of 5 minutes, or when eggs are cooked to your liking.

4. Divide the vegetables among four plates and top each with an egg. Serve more harissa on the side.

No parsnips? Add some extra celeriac. No celeriac? Make up the difference with more sweet potato or even white potato. Speaking of sweet potatoes, garnet yams or Japanese sweet potatoes work best because of their firm texture and great flavor.

Because different harissas vary widely in spiciness by brand and type (sauce is better than paste here), start with less and add more at the end if you want more heat.

All eggs poach a little differently, but letting them sit in hot water still in their shells for a minute helps hold the egg white together when it hits the poaching water.

Use the convection setting (if you have one) at 450°F to help with the final browning. Otherwise, just cook until everything is well browned.

SERVES 4 TO 6

OKONOMIYAKI (CRISPY VEG PANCAKE) WITH SHRIMP

This decidedly nontraditional version of the justifiably famous Japanese street food uses only supermarket ingredients. The veggie-packed pancake is one of those clean-out-the-fridge, make-anytime meals that will immediately become part of your regular rotation the instant you try it. Cabbage is the traditional vegetable choice, but I like to use its younger, greener cousin, Brussels sprouts. Omit the shrimp for a vegetarian version or add bacon for a meaty one. After you've followed this recipe once, you can use whatever ingredients you have to make it "as you like it" (*okonomi*) and cook it on a griddle (*yaki*).

For the batter

¹/₂ cup all-purpose flour

1 teaspoon baking powder

1 teaspoon granulated sugar

³/₄ teaspoon kosher salt

¹/₂ cup instant dashi, vegetable stock (page 226), chicken stock, or water

3 large eggs

For the filling

2 to 3 tablespoons vegetable oil, divided

6 to 8 ounces shiitake mushrooms, stemmed and sliced

Kosher salt

3 cups finely shredded Brussels sprouts or cabbage

1 large carrot, grated (optional)

2 scallions, thinly sliced

6 ounces medium shrimp, peeled and deveined, or rock shrimp

For the sauce

2 tablespoons ketchup

2 tablespoons oyster sauce

2 tablespoons Worcestershire sauce

For the toppings

Kewpie mayonnaise or regular mayo thinned with rice wine vinegar

Toasted sesame seeds

1 sheet nori

Instructions

1. **To make the batter:** Heat the oven to 350°F. Whisk together the flour, baking powder, sugar, and salt. Slowly whisk in the dashi, stock, or water and continue whisking until smooth. Add the eggs and whisk until smooth. There may be a few lumps, but that's OK. Refrigerate while prepping the vegetables.

2. **To make the filling:** Heat a medium (10-inch) nonstick skillet with an ovenproof handle over high heat. Add 1 tablespoon of the oil, the mushrooms, and a big pinch of salt. Cook, tossing frequently, for about 5 minutes until wilted and starting to brown. Set aside on a plate and rinse the skillet out with cold water.

3. Remove the batter from the refrigerator and add the Brussels sprouts or cabbage, mushrooms, carrot, scallions, and shrimp and fold in using a rubber spatula until thoroughly combined.

4. **To cook the pancake:** Heat the skillet over medium-low heat and add 1 tablespoon of the oil. Add the batter and press down with a rubber spatula to compact the mixture. Cook for 7 to 8 minutes, or until the bottom is brown (use the spatula to peek underneath). Slide onto a dinner plate and add another tablespoon of the oil to the pan. Top the pancake with a second plate, invert, and slide the pancake back into the pan. Press down gently again. Cook for 6 to 8 minutes on the second side and transfer to the oven for 10 minutes to cook through.

5. Slide the pancake out onto a serving plate.

6. **Make the sauce:** Mix the ketchup, oyster sauce, and Worcestershire sauce together.

7. **To serve:** Drizzle the pancake with the mayo and the sauce. Sprinkle with sesame seeds. Holding the nori sheet with a pair of tongs, toast it directly over a gas flame until a shade darker and crispy; be careful not to burn it. You can also do this directly under a broiler, with a rack set 6 inches away. Crumble the sheet of nori over top of the pancake and serve immediately.

The traditional broth for okonomiyaki is dashi, the savory broth made from a piece of kombu and bonito flakes. Many Japanese cooks use powdered instant dashi, but if you don't have it, you can use any kind of stock or even plain water. I sometimes add a spoonful of porcini powder or a splash of a vegan seasoning sauce like Yondu to the batter.

VEG FORWARD

SERVES 4

STUFFED SPAGHETTI SQUASH

When it's baked, the flesh of spaghetti squash separates into delicate, fluffy strands that are ideally suited to mixing with flavorful ingredients—in this case a combo of fennel, shiitakes, tomatoes, cheese, and cooked grain. This is a version of a standby dinner I've been making for years.

Ingredients

2 small spaghetti squash (about 1 1/2 to 2 pounds each)

1 tablespoon olive oil, plus more for drizzling

Kosher salt and freshly ground pepper

1 medium onion, chopped

1/2 bulb fennel, chopped

8 shiitake mushroom caps, sliced

1/2 bunch broccolini, chopped (about 1 cup/4 ounces)

1 1/2 cups chopped Slow-Roasted Tomatoes (page 216) or store-bought marinara sauce

1/4 cup water as needed

1 cup cooked freekeh, bulgur, quinoa, farro, or brown rice

1/2 teaspoon smoked paprika

Red pepper flakes

1/2 cup/2 ounces fontina cheese, grated

Instructions

1. Heat the oven to 375°F. Carefully cut the squash in half lengthwise. Scoop out the seeds (I like to use a cookie or ice cream scoop). Drizzle with olive oil and season with salt and pepper.

2. Bake, cut side down, on a small foil-lined baking sheet for 30 to 40 minutes until the tops of the shells are starting to brown and feel soft when pressed lightly with the tip of a knife. Remove from the oven and let cool upside down for 10 minutes to steam.

3. Meanwhile, heat the tablespoon of oil in a large skillet over medium heat. Add the onion and cook until starting to soften, 5 to 6 minutes. Add the fennel and cook for 3 to 4 minutes longer. Add the mushrooms, season with salt and pepper, and cook for 7 to 8 minutes, until they have softened and started to brown. Lower the heat if necessary to keep the onions from scorching.

4. Add the broccolini and tomatoes or marinara and 1/4 cup water if the mixture looks at all dry. Cook for 2 to 3 minutes, stirring.

5. Add the grain to the vegetable mixture and use a fork to scrape the squash out directly into the pan, reserving the shells. Adjust the seasonings and add the smoked paprika and a big pinch of red pepper flakes. Mix well with a fork.

6. Arrange the shells on the same baking sheet, and divide the mixture evenly among them, packing it in and piling it up. Sprinkle with the cheese. Return to the oven and bake for 20 minutes until the cheese is melted at the edges.

The squash can be assembled a day or two ahead and refrigerated until ready to bake. Remove from the fridge 30 minutes before baking and increase the baking time to 30 to 35 minutes.

SERVES 6 TO 8

CARAMELIZED ONION AND POTATO GALETTE

This glorious tart would be a good thing to have in the oven when dinner guests arrive, because the aroma is intoxicating, with flavor to match. The combination of flaky, buttery pastry, deeply flavored and creamy-soft caramelized onions, slightly crispy potatoes, creamy goat cheese, and nutty Gruyère is ridiculously good.

For the dough

1 1/2 cups/192 g all-purpose flour

1 teaspoon granulated sugar

1/2 teaspoon kosher salt

1/4 teaspoon freshly ground pepper

1/2 cup/28 g grated Parmesan cheese

10 tablespoons/140 g (1 stick plus 2 tablespoons) ice-cold unsalted butter, cut into pieces

4 to 5 tablespoons ice water

For the galette

4 ounces soft goat cheese

1 batch Caramelized Onions (page 219), cooled

3 to 4 small potatoes (like fingerlings)

1 teaspoon olive oil

Kosher salt

3 ounces grated Gruyère cheese

1 tablespoon fresh thyme leaves

Freshly ground pepper

Instructions

1. **To make the dough:** Combine the flour, sugar, salt, pepper, and Parmesan cheese in a food processor and pulse to combine. Add the butter and pulse to break it down into smaller pieces. Transfer the mixture to a bowl and continue squeezing the butter through your fingers to flatten the pieces. Using a fork, stir the mixture while dribbling in the water, starting with 4 tablespoons and adding more as needed until you don't see a lot of dry crumbs in the bottom of the bowl and the dough stays together when squeezed. Squeeze it together into a mass in the bowl and transfer to a piece of plastic wrap. Flatten into a disk. Pat the edges together a little to neaten them up and chill for at least 1 hour until firm.

2. Heat the oven to 400°F and line a baking sheet with parchment. On a generously floured surface, roll the dough out to a slightly more than 1/8-inch thickness to a 14-inch circle, flouring as needed and carefully turning the dough halfway through. Transfer to the baking sheet and chill until firm again (you can pop it in the freezer to speed up the process, but don't leave it in so long that it becomes hard and brittle), about 15 minutes.

3. **To make the galette:** Crumble the goat cheese evenly over the dough, leaving a 2-inch border all around. Top with the onions.

4. Thinly slice the potatoes crosswise using a mandoline or as thinly as possible with a knife and toss with the olive oil and salt to taste. Scatter the potatoes on top, tucking some of them into the onions. Sprinkle the Gruyère, thyme, and pepper on top. Fold the edges over to create a 1 1/2-to-2-inch border all around and bake for 40 to 45 minutes, until the filling is bubbling and the crust is deep golden brown. Let cool briefly, slice, and serve warm or at room temperature.

You can use this as a starting point for almost any vegetable galette. The caramelized onions are a good base, but you could add some precooked kale (tucked under the onions a bit to keep it moist) and thinly sliced winter squash instead of the potatoes. You can use ricotta instead of goat cheese for a milder flavor or just leave the cheese out altogether.

VEG FORWARD

MAKES 16 CUPS (1 GALLON)

VEGETARIAN BORSCHT WITH BELUGA LENTILS

This garnet-hued soup brightens up a winter day with its stunning color and tart flavor. It's essential for a borscht to have a certain amount of acidity, and sweetness too, which gives it its signature flavor profile. This makes a big batch, but it freezes beautifully.

Ingredients

1 tablespoon olive oil

1 large onion, finely diced

1 teaspoon kosher salt, or more to taste, divided

4 garlic cloves, minced

1/2 head green cabbage, cored and finely shredded using a food processor

1 tablespoon tomato paste

1 teaspoon sweet paprika

1/4 teaspoon ground allspice

1 pound beets (3 large or 4 medium), peeled and grated using a food processor

3 to 4 large carrots, peeled and grated using a food processor

1 large or 2 small Yukon Gold potatoes, peeled and diced into 1/2-inch cubes

1/2 cup beluga or small green (Puy) lentils

10 cups vegetable stock (page 226)

1/4 cup red wine vinegar, plus more to taste

2 teaspoons sugar

Sour cream or Greek yogurt for serving

1/2 cup chopped dill, plus more for serving

Lemon wedges for serving

Instructions

1. Heat a large soup pot over medium-low heat, and add the oil, followed by the onion, 1/2 teaspoon of the salt, and garlic. Cook, stirring frequently, until softened and starting to turn golden, 8 to 10 minutes. Add the cabbage and remaining 1/2 teaspoon salt. Stir and cook for 3 to 4 minutes, until wilted.

2. Add the tomato paste, paprika, and allspice and cook, stirring, for 2 minutes. Add the beets, carrots, potatoes, lentils, and stock, and bring to a boil over high heat. Reduce to a simmer, cover partially (leave it a crack open), and cook 20 to 25 minutes, or until the lentils and potatoes are tender.

3. Add the vinegar and sugar and adjust the seasonings as needed with salt and pepper, and add more vinegar if needed. Serve hot with sour cream or yogurt, dill, and lemon wedges.

Avoid large, brown lentils. Or add a can of cannellini or butter beans instead.

This recipe makes a lot, and the soup freezes perfectly, so portion it out and save it for a rainy day. It will keep well in the fridge for 4 days.

VEG FORWARD

191

SERVES 4

CITRUS SALAD WITH GREEN OLIVES, BURRATA, AND HONEY-ROASTED PISTACHIOS

With its sunny citrus and vivid green olives, this salad is a bright spot at a dull time of year. It's optimal to use at least two varieties of citrus, so you get a mix of colors and flavors, but even regular navel oranges are fine. Burrata dolloped onto the plate contributes a decadent creaminess that blends with the tangy flavors of the citrus and the olives. Add the fresh snap of fennel and endive and the crunch of honey-roasted pistachios, and you'll have a salad that throws a great party in your mouth.

For the nuts

1 large egg white

2 tablespoons honey

1 teaspoon olive oil

1/4 teaspoon cayenne pepper (or a little less if you don't like spicy)

3 ounces/85 g raw pistachios (heaping 1/2 cup)

1/4 teaspoon kosher salt, or more to taste

For the salad

1/2 to 3/4 of a large fennel bulb, fronds reserved

1 head Belgian endive

3 medium or 4 small oranges, like Cara Cara, blood oranges, Minneola tangelos, navel, or a mix

12 Castelvetrano olives, pitted

2 tablespoons lemon juice

3 tablespoons extra-virgin olive oil

Kosher salt and freshly ground pepper

8 ounces burrata cheese

Instructions

1. **To make the nuts:** Heat the oven to 350°F and line a small baking sheet with parchment. Beat the egg white in a small bowl with a fork until foamy. Mix in the honey, oil, and cayenne. Add the nuts and stir to coat. Transfer to the baking sheet (the nuts will be in a big puddle—that's what you want) and bake for 25 to 30 minutes, removing the nuts from the oven every 5 minutes to stir with a spatula and spread out. After the first 10 minutes, sprinkle with the salt.

2. When the nuts are done, pull the parchment off the pan and let cool completely on the counter. They will crisp up as they cool. If not using right away, store in an airtight container for up to 2 weeks.

3. **To make the salad:** Trim the fennel and cut into quarters. Shave thinly using a mandoline. Alternatively, slice as thinly as possible by hand. Trim the root end of the endive and cut into long, thin pieces. Trim the pith and peel from the oranges and slice into rounds. Tear the olives into large pieces.

4. In a small bowl, use a fork to mix together the lemon juice, olive oil, and salt and pepper to taste.

5. Assemble individual salads on plates, starting with the fennel and endive, followed by the oranges and olives. Drizzle the dressing over top, using only what you need and serving any extra on the side. Sprinkle with the nuts, fennel fronds, and salt and pepper to taste.

6. Dollop a generous spoonful of burrata on the side of each plate and serve.

SERVES 4

TARDIVO WITH WARM ANCHOVY DRESSING, WALNUTS, AND GORGONZOLA

This anchovy dressing is so well balanced that I would urge you to feed it to people who claim to hate anchovies. It beautifully complements the blue cheese and walnuts, all atop crunchy, chilled spears of Tardivo. Tardivo is a forced radicchio with a dramatic appearance. It's sweeter than radicchio, so if you can't find it, try using Belgian endive for this salad instead. They are similar in texture and flavor. Another mild radicchio like Castelfranco would work well too.

For the dressing

3 tablespoons extra-virgin olive oil

2 large garlic cloves, minced

6 to 8 anchovy filets

2 tablespoons lemon juice

2 teaspoons Dijon mustard

2 teaspoons aged balsamic vinegar

Kosher salt and freshly ground pepper

For the salad

1 head mild radicchio (8 ounces), such as Tardivo or Castelfranco

1 1/2 ounces gorgonzola or other mild blue cheese (scant 1/4 cup)

1/3 cup/1 ounce walnuts

Flaky salt and freshly ground pepper

Instructions

1. **To make the dressing:** Heat the oil in a small skillet over medium-low heat. Add the garlic and cook until just starting to take on color, about 2 to 3 minutes. Add the anchovies and cook for 1 to 2 minutes longer, until the garlic is toasted and golden brown, smashing the anchovies with a wooden spoon to help them dissolve into the oil.

2. Whisk in the lemon juice, mustard, and vinegar. Season with salt and pepper to taste. Thin with a small amount of water if needed.

3. **To make the salad:** Place the radicchio in a bowl and toss with the dressing. Top with the blue cheese and the walnuts. Season lightly with flaky salt and pepper and serve.

Crisp romaine hearts are also good in this salad, as are other kinds of radicchio and endive.

The dressing is terrific on other things, such as scallops and roasted broccoli.

VEG FORWARD

SERVES 4

SHEET-PAN BRAISED FENNEL WITH PARM AND HAZELNUTS

This recipe has a short ingredient list but is long on flavor. Cooked fennel has an entirely different character than raw, which has a more pronounced anise taste. Here, it becomes more of a background note, and the fennel wedges turn sweet and jammy as they braise happily on a sheet pan, making this dish easy to make. Leftovers keep well and make a great flavor base for a simple pasta dish.

Ingredients

3 large or 4 medium fennel bulbs (about 3 pounds)

1/4 cup hazelnuts

2 tablespoons olive oil

1/2 teaspoon kosher salt

Freshly ground pepper

1 cup chicken or vegetable stock (page 226)

1 tablespoon fresh thyme leaves, roughly chopped

1/2 fluffy cup Parmesan cheese (about 1/2 ounce)

Instructions

1. Heat the oven to 450°F. Cut the tops off the fennel bulbs and wash and dry. Reserve the fronds if they are in good shape. Trim the very bottom of the bulbs, keeping the core intact. Cut each bulb into 8 wedges.

2. Bake the hazelnuts for 8 to 10 minutes, until they smell toasty, the skins are popping off, and they are turning golden, rolling them around once or twice. Remove from the oven and tip into a bowl. Cover the bowl with a folded dishcloth and let the nuts cool. Rub off as much of the hazelnut skins as you can, the parts that comes off easily. Separate the nuts from the skins and discard the skins. Very coarsely chop the nuts and set aside.

3. Place the fennel on a baking sheet and toss with the oil, salt, and pepper, using your hands to coat everything well. Spread out evenly, crowding more at the edges than in the center to encourage browning.

4. Place in the oven and roast for 40 to 45 minutes. At this point most of the fennel pieces should be browning on the bottom. If not, give it a few more minutes. Gently turn each piece using tongs or a spatula and cook for 10 minutes longer.

5. Reduce the oven temperature to 400°F. Pour the stock over the fennel, tipping the pan back and forth to distribute the liquid evenly, especially into the corners. Sprinkle with the thyme leaves and the Parmesan.

6. Cook until the liquid has mostly evaporated, about 20 minutes, tipping the pan a few times during cooking to redistribute the liquid.

7. Sprinkle the fennel with the reserved fennel fronds (if you have them) and serve.

If you don't want to bother with toasting and skinning the hazelnuts, you can use whole roasted almonds.

SERVES 4

SMASHED JAPANESE SWEET POTATOES WITH NORI

Japanese sweet potatoes have purple skin and pale, creamy flesh, which turns a buttery yellow when cooked. They're so good plain that they don't really need much embellishment. Their texture is drier and fluffier than a regular sweet potato. This simple treatment makes them even better. These are salty-sweet and crispy as hell.

Ingredients

4 small or 2 large Japanese sweet potatoes (about 1 ½ pounds)

Kosher salt

1 sheet nori

Vegetable oil for the pan

2 tablespoons butter, melted

Flaky salt

Instructions

1. Heat the oven to 425°F. Cut the pointy tips off the potatoes and cut them into 1 ½-inch rounds. You'll get 3 to 4 slices out of each one, depending on their size.

2. Place the potatoes in a medium saucepan and cover with an inch or two of cold salted water. Bring to a boil over high heat, reduce to a simmer, and cook for 15 to 20 minutes, until tender. The tip of a paring knife should slide right into the center of a larger piece. Drain in a colander and let cool slightly.

3. Hold the sheet of nori with a pair of tongs and wave directly over a gas flame until it begins to buckle, smell toasty, and become crisp. You can also do this directly under a broiler with a rack set 6 inches away. Watch very carefully to make sure it doesn't burn. Once it's cool, tear into small pieces like you're tearing up a piece of paper.

4. Lightly oil a baking sheet. Transfer the potato slices one at a time to the baking sheet and use the heel of your hand to gently press down on the potato slice until it spreads out and cracks on the edges. (Alternatively, use the flat bottom of a sturdy drinking glass.)

5. Brush the tops with butter and sprinkle with half the nori. Carefully turn each slice using a spatula and brush the other side with the remaining butter and sprinkle with remaining nori.

6. Bake for 20 to 25 minutes, until deeply golden on the undersides. Carefully turn each potato slice and bake for 15 to 20 minutes longer until they are golden brown all over. Sprinkle with flaky salt and serve immediately.

Smaller sweet potatoes will work better for this recipe, but big ones work too—they will just become rather large in diameter by the time you smash them. If they break apart a little, don't fret—it just means more crispy bits to enjoy.

The potatoes reheat well. Just pop them into a 425°F oven for about 15 minutes until heated through, or simply heat in the microwave.

VEG FORWARD

201

SERVES 6 TO 8

APPLE CONFIT CAKE

Paper-thin apple slices shingled with sprinklings of sugar meld together during 3 hours of slow and gentle cooking, which is when the magic happens. The caramel that lines the pan melts and permeates the apples, creating an intricately layered, soft brick of pure apple flavor. This dessert has none of the richness of tarte Tatin, which it might remind you of, because the apples aren't drenched in butter. After the apples are cooked, a thin layer of cake batter is added to bake right on top of the fruit, balancing the fruit layer. Most of the working time is hands-off, but you'll want to make this on a day when you'll be around the house, since it does take a while. I promise you it's worth every minute!

For the apples

3/4 cup/151 g granulated sugar, divided

2 tablespoons water

4 to 6 small Granny Smith apples (2 to 2 1/4 pounds)

For the cake

3/4 cup/96 g all-purpose flour

1/2 teaspoon baking powder

1/4 teaspoon kosher salt

1/4 teaspoon ground cardamom

4 tablespoons/56 g unsalted butter (1/2 stick), softened

1/2 cup/101 g granulated sugar

1 large egg, at room temperature

1/2 teaspoon vanilla extract

1/4 cup whole milk

For serving

Whipped cream or vanilla ice cream

Instructions

1. **To make the apples:** Have a standard (8-by-4-inch) loaf pan at the ready. Combine 1/2 cup/101 g of the sugar with the water in a small saucepan or medium skillet. Stir until the sugar is moistened. Cook over medium-high heat, carefully and gently swirling but not stirring, until the sugar starts to turn golden. Use a pastry brush dipped in water to dissolve any sugar crystals clinging to the sides. Once it starts to color, reduce the heat to medium-low so you can control the cooking better. Continue cooking until the caramel turns a deep amber color; wisps of smoke will rise from the surface. As soon as it reaches the right color, quickly and carefully pour into the loaf pan and set it aside.

2. Heat the oven to 350°F, with a rack in the middle. Peel the apples and cut them in half. Use a melon baller or small spoon to scoop out the seeds. With a vegetable peeler, trim the ends and remove any stems. Slice the apples 1/8 inch thick using a mandoline or sharp knife.

3. Place the remaining 1/4 cup/50 g sugar in a small bowl. Position the pan vertically in front of you. Shingle the apple slices, starting at the end of the pan nearest you, and layer them away from you, aiming to create an overlapping fish scale pattern, one layer at a time. Sprinkle the first layer with 1 teaspoon of the sugar. Continue in this way, layering the apples and sprinkling with the sugar (don't worry about the pattern of the apple slices after the first layer, just try to keep them even). Every few layers, gently press down, feeling for any low or uneven spots and evening them up, especially toward the edges.

4. When the pan is about three quarters full (this will be about 9 layers of sliced apples), you should have used most of the apples and sugar. Make sure to leave at least 1 inch of space at the top for the cake batter, even though you may not have used all the apples. Sprinkle any remaining sugar over top. Cover the pan with foil and tightly crimp it around the edges. Place the pan in a small roasting pan (like a 9-by-13-inch pan) and pour enough very hot tap water in the pan to come about halfway up the sides of the loaf pan.

5. Bake for 1 hour. Remove from the oven, remove the foil, and press down gently with a spatula so that the juices run over top of the apples. Reduce the oven temperature to 300°F and return the covered pan to the oven for another hour.

6. Remove the pan from the oven and press down as you did before. Return to the oven, uncovered and still in the water bath, and bake for 30 minutes longer.

7. **Meanwhile, make the cake:** Whisk together the flour, baking powder, salt, and cardamom in a small bowl. Cream the butter and sugar together in the bowl of a stand mixer with the paddle attachment on medium-high speed or in a large bowl with a hand mixer until fluffy. Beat in the egg and vanilla. Reduce the mixer speed to low and add a third of the dry ingredients, followed by half of the milk. Add another third of the dry ingredients, followed by the remaining milk. Beat in the remaining dry ingredients, mixing just until it's incorporated, scraping the bowl and beater as needed.

8. Remove the pan with the apples from the oven and turn the oven heat up to 350°F. Place the pan on a foil-lined baking sheet and top the apples with the cake batter, smoothing it with an offset spatula. Return to the oven and bake for 30 to 40 minutes, or until a toothpick inserted in the center comes out clean. Let the cake cool completely on a rack. Cover and leave it out to cool and set, about 3 hours or overnight.

9. When you're ready to serve, put the cake in a 200°F oven for about 10 minutes to loosen the caramel. Run a table knife around the sides, loosening the cake and the apples. Turn the pan upside down on a serving platter and tap gently on the bottom of the pan until you feel the cake slide out. If necessary, use the table knife to help nudge it out. Cut into 1-inch-thick slices and serve with whipped cream or ice cream if desired.

Although you could serve the cake on the day you make it, I find it much easier to make it the day before I want to serve it, since it takes a lot of passive time to make and it benefits from a long cooling time.

ESSENTIALS

VEG FORWARD

OVEN-BAKED POLENTA
Serves 4 to 6

This creamy porridge goes well with Mushroom Bourguignon (page 177). Or throw some roasted vegetables on top and call it dinner. It's made with a convenient all-in-the-oven method, which works perfectly, without the need for the constant stirring and the inevitable spitting and spattering of the traditional stovetop version. Don't be skeptical when you add all that water to the baking dish—the polenta will absorb every bit of it. Have faith!

INGREDIENTS
1 cup medium-grind (not instant) polenta (I like Bob's Red Mill corn grits/polenta)
4 cups boiling water
1 teaspoon salt
3/4 cup whole milk, warmed
1 to 2 tablespoons unsalted butter
1/2 ounce Parmesan cheese, grated (1/2 fluffy cup)

INSTRUCTIONS
Preheat the oven to 350°F. Combine the polenta, water, and salt in an 8-by-11-inch (2-quart) baking dish. Place the dish on a foil-lined baking sheet and bake, uncovered, for 30 minutes.

Remove from the oven and stir well using a small whisk to loosen any thickened polenta from the sides and bottom of the dish. Stir in the milk, butter, and cheese until the butter is melted and everything is smooth and well incorporated. Continue baking for 20 minutes longer and stir again. Stir twice more at 10-minute intervals, cooking for a total of 70 minutes. At this point, the polenta should be sufficiently thick and creamy. It will continue to thicken as it cools.

If you want to brown the top, sprinkle with the Parmesan and run under the broiler for a couple minutes. Serve hot.

FRESH PASTA
Makes about 2 pounds; enough for one lasagna and pappardelle for 4

I'm always shocked at how easy making fresh pasta is. It elevates even the simplest sauce—a basil pesto from the garden; brown butter, hazelnuts, and sage; or simply sautéed mushrooms in butter—to a sublime meal. Fresh pasta sheets are the number one option for a stellar tray of lasagna, like the Veggie Bolognese Lasagna on page 175.

A KitchenAid stand mixer does a fine job of mixing the dough, which I then roll out using the pasta attachment (see page xix). An old-fashioned pasta machine works very well too. This recipe will make more than you need for the lasagna, but it's helpful to have extra dough to account for the learning curve. Extra dough can be frozen for future use.

INGREDIENTS
Semolina flour for dusting
About 4 3/4 cups/600 g all-purpose flour
3/4 teaspoon fine sea salt
7 large eggs
1 tablespoon water, if needed

VEG FORWARD

INSTRUCTIONS

Line a baking sheet or two with wax or parchment paper and dust generously with semolina. Set aside. Mix the flour and salt on the lowest speed in the bowl of a stand mixer using the paddle attachment. Add the eggs and mix on speed #2 for 1 to 2 minutes, or until thoroughly combined. If there are dry, crumbly bits in the bottom of the bowl, add the water. Switch to the dough hook and continue mixing at speed #2 for 2 minutes. Scrape the dough out of the bowl and onto an unfloured countertop and continue kneading by hand until very smooth, about 2 minutes. The dough shouldn't be sticky at all. If it's sticky, dust your hands and the surface lightly with flour as you knead. Let dough rest at room temperature, wrapped tightly in plastic, for 30 minutes.

Divide the pasta dough into 4 pieces using a bench scraper or a knife. Remove one piece and tightly wrap the remaining dough. Lightly flour the surface and the piece of dough and form it into a rectangle narrower than the width of the rollers on your pasta machine (about 4 by 7 inches). Roll a few times with a rolling pin until it is about 1/4 inch thick and about 5 by 10 inches, keeping it narrower than the rollers and taking care to keep it rectangular.

Set your pasta machine to the widest setting (#1) and feed the dough through the rollers. Return the dough to your work surface and turn it so it is horizontal as you look at it and fold the sides toward the center, overlapping as needed to form a new rectangle (about 3 1/2 by 6 inches) that is narrower than the rollers. Roll it out again with the rolling pin so it is 1/4 inch thick (and about 4 by 8 inches) and run it through the machine again, still set on the widest setting.

Very lightly flour the dough and set the rollers to the next thinnest setting (#2), and run the dough through the rollers. Continue in this way, narrowing the rollers by one notch for each pass, until you get to setting #6 on a KitchenAid attachment or #5 on an Atlas 150 Marcato hand-cranked pasta machine. Run the dough strips through a second time once you get to the thinnest setting. When the strips become too long (usually after setting #3), cut in half using clean kitchen scissors and continue separately with each piece, adjusting the

rollers as needed and remembering where you left off. Cut in half again after rolling the first time on #6.

Transfer the sheets of pasta to the semolina-dusted baking sheet, and generously sprinkle more semolina over the top. Trim the ends if they are hanging off the ends of the pan. Top with another sheet of wax or parchment and continue in this way until you've used all the dough. Pasta dough can be tightly wrapped and frozen for up to 1 month. Defrost overnight in the refrigerator before using. You can also freeze the sheets. Make sure they are liberally coated with semolina, and fold each sheet a few times. Arrange the folded sheets in an airtight container and freeze until needed.

To make pappardelle noodles: Fold 2 sheets of pasta over a few times until you have a small rectangle. Cut into ribbons, fluff up into little piles, and liberally sprinkle with semolina. Let them dry for an hour or so at room temperature in little "nests" on a baking sheet. Place the baking sheet in the freezer until the pasta is frozen, then transfer to a zip-top bag or airtight container and store in the freezer until needed.

To cook the pasta: Bring a large pot of water to a rolling boil and salt liberally. Add the pasta and cook for about 1 minute. Drain and dress with whatever sauce you're using and serve immediately.

Notes: Use fine sea salt, not kosher, because kosher salt can tear the delicate pasta sheets as they go through the rollers.

Don't be afraid to use plenty of semolina on the finished pasta. It may seem excessive, but it's needed to prevent sticking. It will fall to the bottom of the pot when you cook it.

Use the backs of your hands and arms to handle the strips of dough. Let it drape on the backs of your hands as you feed it through the rollers and catch it on the other side.

If you're making the pasta sheets for lasagna, you might find it easier to freeze them as directed above one day and assemble the lasagna another day.

You can make fettuccine instead of pappardelle if you want to cut it using the pasta machine. Just change the rollers.

VEG FORWARD

PULL-APART FOCACCIA
Serves 8 to 10

This pull-apart version of focaccia brings a sense of fun to the traditional Italian flatbread. It's got to be the easiest homemade bread ever and can turn any veg-based dish into a square meal. Try it alongside End of Summer Vegetable Soup (page 89), Simple Gazpacho (page 83), or Grilled Zucchini with Whipped Ricotta, Calabrian Chili, and Almonds (page 111). As with any yeast dough, you have a lot of flexibility with timing. I find it very easy to mix up the dough a day or two before I want to bake it and just forget about it in the fridge, but if you aren't a planner and want to speed things up, you can make the dough on the same day you want to bake. You can also transfer the dough to the pan in one piece for a traditional focaccia, instead of dividing it for the pull-apart version.

INGREDIENTS
2 1/2 cups/562 g lukewarm water
1 1/2 teaspoons instant dry yeast
5 cups/640 g all-purpose flour
4 teaspoons/12 g kosher salt
6 tablespoons extra-virgin olive oil, divided
1/3 fluffy cup/20 g grated Parmesan cheese
Fresh rosemary
Flaky salt for sprinkling

INSTRUCTIONS
Pour the water into a medium bowl. Sprinkle the yeast over top and stir to combine; let sit for about 5 minutes.

Whisk together the flour and salt in a large bowl. Using a rubber spatula, stir the flour and the salt into the yeast and water mixture, combining thoroughly. Drizzle about a tablespoon of the oil around the edges of the bowl, pick up the mass of dough so you can oil underneath, and turn it over a few times to coat. Drizzle another tablespoon of oil on top, seal tightly with plastic wrap, and refrigerate for at least 12 hours and as many as 48. If you want to bake it the same day, let the dough rise on the counter for 1 1/2 to 2 hours, or until doubled in size.

Dampen your hands and make 4 folds, scooping from underneath and turning the dough over onto itself, turning the bowl a quarter turn each time. This will simultaneously deflate the dough and create some structure.

Pour 2 tablespoons of the oil into a 9-by-13-inch metal baking pan and tilt the pan to spread it out evenly. Scrape the dough out of the bowl and onto the counter-top. Oil your hands lightly using the oil on the surface of the dough, and using a bench scraper, divide the dough into 4 pieces. Then cut each quarter into 5 or 6 pieces. It's not important that they all be the same size. Shape each piece of dough into a tight ball and place in the pan, arranging them randomly with roughly equal amounts of space around the balls. Any gaps will close up as the dough rises.

Cover with an oiled piece of plastic wrap and let rise in a not-too-cold place until doubled, 1 1/2 to 2 1/2 hours. It could take longer if the room is very cold. If you're working with dough that hasn't been refrigerated, this rise will take 1 to 1 1/2 hours.

When you're ready to bake, heat oven to 450°F with an oven rack in the middle. If you have a baking stone or steel, place it on the rack. Drizzle the dough with the remaining 2 tablespoons oil and lightly oil your fingers with it. Dimple the entire surface of the dough deeply, all the way down to the bottom of the pan, as if you were playing a concerto. Sprinkle with the cheese, rosemary, and flaky salt and bake 25 to 30 minutes until deep golden brown on top. As soon as the pan is cool enough to handle, use a spatula to slide out onto a cooling rack so the bottom doesn't get soggy.

PIZZA DOUGH
Makes enough for 2 (12-inch) pizzas

This dough is very soft and has a high proportion of water, which makes for a bubbly, chewy texture when baked. Don't be afraid to use plenty of flour when handling the dough, which will make it easier to work with. Don't incorporate it into the dough; it will toughen it.

INGREDIENTS
1/2 teaspoon active dry yeast
1 1/4 cups/270 g warm water

2 ¹/₃ cups/298 g bread flour or all-purpose flour
1 ¹/₂ teaspoons kosher salt
Olive oil for the bowl

INSTRUCTIONS

Sprinkle yeast over the warm water to dissolve it. Whisk flour and salt in a large bowl. Stir in the yeast mixture until fully incorporated. Cover and let stand for 10 to 15 minutes.

Dampen your hand and give the dough a few turns in the bowl until slightly smooth. Make four "stretch and fold" movements, scooping your hand from under the dough, stretching it up, and folding the dough over on itself. Turn it over and tuck the sides in so you have a smooth, taut ball. Transfer to a clean, oiled bowl, and turn the dough over a few times to make sure the surface is oiled. Cover with plastic wrap and refrigerate overnight or for as long as 3 days. Alternatively, if you want to bake the same day, let the dough rise at room temperature until doubled, about 1 hour.

When you're ready to bake, remove the dough from the fridge about an hour before needed so it can return to room temperature.

Heat the oven to 550°F, or your highest oven setting, with a baking steel or stone inside on the center rack. If using a steel or stone, heat it for 45 minutes. If you don't have a steel or stone, heat a baking sheet, upside down, on the middle rack for at least 15 minutes.

Scrape the dough out of the bowl onto a generously floured surface. Divide into 2 roughly equal pieces, handling the dough as little as possible. Cut a 12-inch sheet of parchment, spray or brush with olive oil, and place on a pizza peel or the back side of another rimmed baking sheet or a rimless cookie sheet.

Transfer one piece of dough to the parchment and, with floured hands, gently stretch into a roughly 12-inch circle. Top as desired and slide the dough (still on the parchment) onto the steel, stone, or baking sheet.

Bake for about 10 minutes, until the crust is well browned on the edges and the cheese is bubbling. Use the peel or cookie sheet to scoop up the pizza, giving a

little tug on the paper to help if needed, and transfer to a serving board. Repeat with the second piece of dough.

SOCCA (CHICKPEA PANCAKES)
Makes 2 thicker pancakes or 3 thinner ones

The main ingredient of this stupidly simple home version of the Provençal street snack socca is chickpea flour, which, happily, has become widely available due to the popularity of gluten-free baking. Torn into pieces, the savory pancakes can be served with chilled rosé or topped with the Roasted Ratatouille on page 63, cut into wedges, and eaten like pizza. Thicker pancakes will stand up better to toppings, especially if they're on the heavy side, while the thinner ones are best for eating on their own. Parmesan is not traditional, but it adds a certain je ne sais quoi that I prefer. Feel free to leave it out.

INGREDIENTS

1 cup/101 g chickpea (garbanzo) flour
1 cup water
¹/₂ cup lightly packed (20 g) finely grated Parmesan
2 tablespoons olive oil, plus more for cooking
³/₄ teaspoon kosher salt
Freshly ground pepper

INSTRUCTIONS

Whisk together the chickpea flour, water, Parmesan, oil, salt, and pepper until smooth. Cover with plastic and let rest for at least 30 minutes at room temperature. The batter can rest for up to 1 day, refrigerated.

Heat the broiler, with a rack 8 inches away. Then heat a 9- or 10-inch cast-iron skillet in the oven for about 5 minutes. Add 1 tablespoon oil to the pan and pour in about a third of the batter (scant ¹/₂ cup) for a thinner pancake or half the batter (³/₄ cup) for a thicker one, tilting the pan to cover the bottom evenly. Return to the oven and cook until the pancake is blistered and browned on top, about 6 minutes for thinner socca and 7 minutes for thicker ones.

Slide the pancake onto a plate, reheat the pan for a few minutes, and repeat with the remaining batter.

Notes: If you don't have a broiler, you can make these

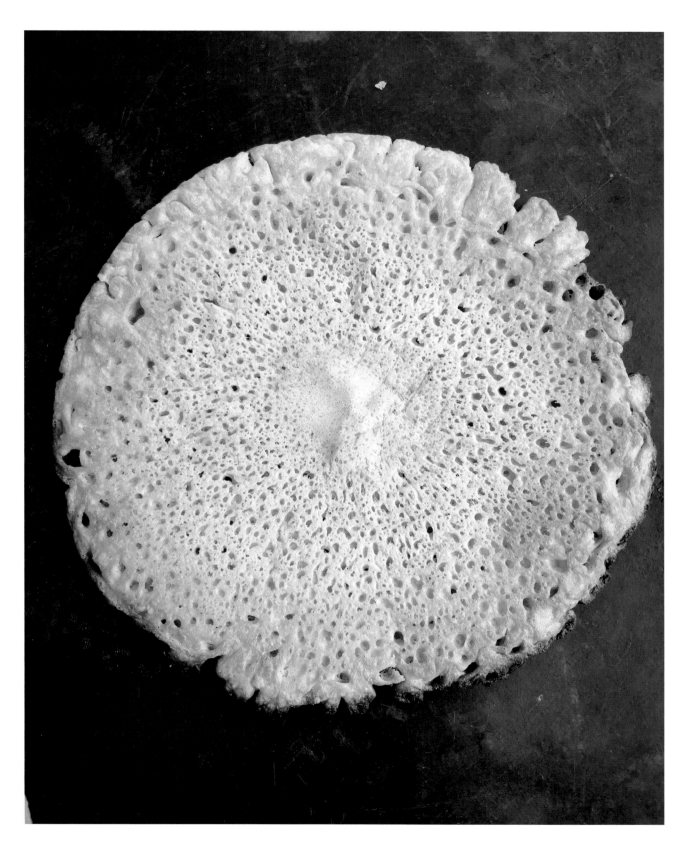

on the stovetop, provided you make thin pancakes. (It's too difficult to flip thicker ones.) Heat the skillet until moderately hot over medium heat. Add 1 tablespoon olive oil and pour in the batter, tilting the pan to cover the bottom. For thinner pancakes, cook for 3 minutes on the first side and 1 minute on the second side.

HOMEMADE CORN TORTILLAS
Makes 20 (5-inch) tortillas

Making homemade tortillas isn't as difficult as you might think, and it's so worth the effort for not only the flavor but the texture too. They're the centerpiece for a taco spread like the one on page 133. Masa harina, which is made from nixtamalized corn (it's totally different from cornmeal—don't confuse the two) is available in most supermarkets, or you can order masa harina made from heirloom varieties of corn online. I particularly like the look of blue corn tortillas, and I like to serve a mix for a taco spread.

INGREDIENTS
2 cups/230 g masa harina
1 1/2 cups warm water
1/2 teaspoon kosher salt

INSTRUCTIONS
In a large, wide bowl, use your hands to combine the masa harina and water. Knead the mixture around the bowl for 2 minutes to form a smooth mass, then transfer to a work surface and continue to knead for a few minutes more. Let the dough rest, covered, for 10 minutes. Knead in a little more water until it feels supple, but not sticky.

Heat a large seasoned or lightly oiled cast-iron skillet or griddle over medium-high heat. Cut open a quart-size zip-top bag. Cut off the top and the sides so you are left with a hinged piece of plastic. Trim it further so it fits neatly inside the press.

Pinch off a golf ball–sized (1.5 ounce) piece of dough and roll between your hands to form a ball. Place the open bag in the center of the press and place the ball of dough in the center. Fold the other half of the bag

over the top. Close the press, using medium pressure so that it forms a 5-inch circle. Don't press so hard that the tortilla becomes too thin to handle (there will be some trial and error involved here).

Gently peel back the top layer of plastic. Flip over so the tortilla is on your palm and peel back the plastic on the other side. Gently toss the tortilla between your hands as you bring it toward the hot pan; this motion will at once slightly stretch the tortilla and keep it from sticking to your hands. Flip your hand over above the skillet so that the tortilla falls flat into it. Cook about 2 minutes on the first side (if the pan is hot enough, it will start to bubble), or until starting to brown in spots. Use a spatula to flip and cook for about 1 minute on the second side. Transfer to a small plate and repeat until all the dough is cooked.

You can press the next tortilla while the previous one cooks, and use two pans or a pancake griddle to speed up the process by cooking two at once. Continue stacking the tortillas on the plate. Serve right away or wrap in plastic and refrigerate until needed. Serve warm. Wrap in foil and heat in a 200°F oven before serving.

SALSA MACHA
Makes 2 cups

Salsa macha is Mexico's version of Asian chili crisp. It's an ode to chilies, packed with dried ones that have been toasted in oil, along with garlic, salted peanuts, and sesame seeds. That's all ground into a rich, oily condiment that adds heat and smoky savoriness to everything it touches. It's especially good as a condiment on Cauliflower-Pepita Tacos (page 133) and Green Veggie Enchiladas (page 127), but I love it on scrambled eggs, roasted vegetables, or in a bowl of soup or my grain bowl du jour, and much more.

INGREDIENTS
1 1/2 cups vegetable oil, preferably grapeseed or safflower oil
4 to 6 garlic cloves, sliced
3/4 cup classic cocktail peanuts
2 tablespoons sesame seeds
2 ounces mixed dried chilies, such as ancho, pasilla,

VEG FORWARD

guajillo, and chile de árbol, stemmed, seeded, and torn into 1-inch pieces

1 tablespoon vinegar, such as white wine, apple cider, or rice wine

1 teaspoon brown sugar

1 teaspoon kosher salt, or more to taste

INSTRUCTIONS

Heat the oil in a wide saucepan over medium heat. Put 1 slice of garlic in the saucepan and when it sizzles, add the rest of the garlic. Cook, stirring with a wooden spoon, for 2 to 3 minutes, until the garlic is just starting to brown around the edges.

Add the peanuts and sesame seeds and cook for 1 to 2 minutes longer, stirring, or until the garlic is light golden brown.

Add the chilies, pushing them under the oil, and turn off the heat. They will sizzle and cook even though the heat is off. Stir a few times until the sizzling stops.

Let cool completely and transfer to a food processor (you can also use an immersion blender and process carefully right in the pan). Pulse until everything is roughly chopped but not pureed. You want texture and crunch. Add the vinegar, brown sugar, and salt. Transfer to a jar and store in the refrigerator. It will keep for at least 3 months as long as you keep the top slicked with oil.

Notes: You can use whatever combination of dried chilies you want. Since they vary a lot in size, it's best to put them on the scale (before prepping them) to get the right amount. I use 2 pasilla, 2 guajillo, 2 ancho, and 4 chiles de árbol. Most of the heat comes from the tiny árbol chilies, so if you want more heat, use more of those. They don't affect the total weight because they're so small.

SLOW-ROASTED TOMATOES
Makes 2 to 3 dozen halves

There is nothing quite like the flavor of slow-roasted tomatoes, not to mention the heady aroma that fills the house. As the moisture is slowly cooked out of the tomatoes, the flavors concentrate, and they are coaxed into jammy perfection. Pop them into soups, stews, and pastas, like Farro and Sweet Red Pepper Bake (page 55) or Stuffed Spaghetti Squash (page 55), or Greek Slab Sandwich (page 53). You can also freeze them for use throughout the year to bring a little sunshine to the cooler months. Any kind of tomato can be cooked this way, including tiny cherry tomatoes, but plum tomatoes, sometimes called sauce tomatoes, are the best. If the skins of the tomatoes are thin, you can eat them, especially if you're adding them to toast or pizza, but you can easily slip the skins off after they're cooked too.

INGREDIENTS

3 large garlic cloves, grated on a Microplane

3 tablespoons olive oil

14 to 16 plum tomatoes, halved lengthwise

1 teaspoon kosher salt

Freshly ground pepper

1 tablespoon fresh thyme leaves

1 tablespoon Aleppo-style pepper (optional)

INSTRUCTIONS

Heat the oven to 300°F, with a rack in the middle. Line a baking sheet with parchment paper. Mix the garlic with the oil in a small bowl.

Arrange the tomatoes close together, with the cut sides up. If any are very large, quarter them. Season with the salt (use a little more if needed to sprinkle everything evenly) and an even sprinkling of pepper. Brush them with the garlic oil, taking care to distribute the garlic evenly with the brush. Sprinkle the thyme leaves over top.

Bake until the tomatoes are shriveled but still a bit juicy and the juices on the parchment start to darken, 1 1/2 hours for small tomatoes to 2 1/2 hours for larger tomatoes, but use your own judgment. If you want to make a spicy version, add the Aleppo-style pepper after the first hour.

Let the tomatoes cool on the baking sheet. The juices will thicken, and they'll be easier to handle when they're cool.

Once they've cooled, layer them in a flat container with wax paper or parchment between the layers. Chill in the refrigerator, and once cold, freeze for later use. Or just store in the refrigerator for up to 5 days.

Notes: Cooking times will vary according to the size and juiciness of the tomatoes you use.

Chilling the tomatoes before putting them in the freezer reduces the amount of ice crystals that form in the container. When you're ready to use them, defrost as many as you need on a plate at room temperature. They will exude some extra liquid, which you can blot with a paper towel or cook off.

BIG BATCH ROASTED GARLIC
Makes 1/3 to 3/4 cup, depending on the size of the garlic

Sure, you can roast just one head of garlic, but every time I make a big batch, it's gone within a week. I squeeze all the cloves into a bowl and scrape them into a jar. I especially like to use it to amp up the flavor of uncooked things like vinaigrettes, where raw garlic can be overpowering. It's also a time-saver; instead of chopping garlic every time you need it, just spoon some roasted garlic into the pan instead.

INGREDIENTS
4 large heads garlic
Olive oil, for drizzling

INSTRUCTIONS

Heat the oven to 400°F. Line a small baking sheet or cast-iron skillet with a large square of foil. Place the garlic heads close together but not touching on the foil and drizzle generously with oil. Bundle up the foil, making a loose package that's tightly sealed. Roast for 1 hour and 20 minutes, or until the skins are turning golden brown and the garlic cloves are very soft. Let cool.

Trim the tops off each head with a sharp serrated knife and squeeze the garlic into a glass jar or container. It will keep in the refrigerator for about a week, longer if you keep it covered in a layer of oil.

Notes: If you roast just one garlic head, reduce the cooking time to about an hour.

Use roasted garlic anywhere you would use fresh garlic to get a more mellow flavor. Mix into any pasta sauce instead of fresh garlic, add some to mayo for an instant aioli, whisk some into vinaigrette for extra oomph, or stir some into soups for a deeper umami flavor.

SIMPLE CHUNKY TOMATO SAUCE
Makes about 4 cups

Quick to make, this homemade tomato sauce has a fresher, brighter flavor than jarred sauce. It's purposely on the thinner side, making it the right consistency for the Eggplant Parm and Pasta Bake on page 131, but if you want the sauce a bit thicker for, say, pizza, just cook it a little longer.

INGREDIENTS
2 tablespoons olive oil
1 large onion, diced
4 to 6 garlic cloves, thinly sliced
2 (28-ounce) cans whole San Marzano tomatoes
2 cups water
1/2 teaspoon kosher salt
1/4 teaspoon red pepper flakes or more to taste
Freshly ground pepper
4 to 6 fresh basil leaves, torn

VEG FORWARD

217

INSTRUCTIONS

Heat a large (12-inch) skillet or small Dutch oven over medium heat. Add the oil, followed by the onion and garlic. Cook, stirring occasionally, for 8 to 10 minutes, until light golden.

Break up the tomatoes over a large bowl, using your hands, removing the cores as you go. Add the tomatoes and water (rinse out the can or box) and bring to a boil.

Lower the heat to maintain a low, steady simmer. Add the salt, red pepper flakes, black pepper to taste, and the basil. Simmer for 25 to 30 minutes, until slightly thickened but still a little loose. The sauce can be refrigerated for up to 4 days, or frozen for several months.

CARAMELIZED ONIONS
Makes about 2 1/2 cups

Keep a batch of these deliciously sweet onions in the fridge where they will find their way into all kinds of dishes: morning eggs; quick pastas; roasted potatoes; or on top of burgers, pizzas, and focaccia. Many recipes and techniques claim to be the best or the only way to caramelize onions. This is the method that works for me. First, get good color on the onions, stopping just short of burning them. Then, add water (and, if you like, Madeira or other spirits for flavor) to deglaze the pan and give the onions some liquid to loll around in. Pay attention to the cues given in the recipe, and in general, err on the side of aggressive heat to make sure you get the initial color you need on the onions; you can always turn the heat down later.

INGREDIENTS

4 large Spanish onions (2 to 3 pounds)
1 tablespoon olive oil
1 tablespoon unsalted butter
3/4 teaspoon kosher salt
1/4 to 1/2 cup water, plus more as needed
1/4 cup Madeira, dry sherry, or cognac (optional)
Freshly ground pepper

INSTRUCTIONS
Slice the onions in half lengthwise (from root to stem end), peel them, and slice them lengthwise about 1/4 inch thick (in the same direction).

Heat a large (12-inch) skillet over medium-high heat and add the oil and the butter. Add the onions and salt and toss gently, using tongs. If the onions are steaming and not browning after the first 5 minutes, turn the heat up to high. Cook for 10 to 12 minutes, stirring only occasionally so the onions have a chance to brown, by which time they should be soft and wilted and starting to turn brown all over.

Add 1/4 cup of the water and the Madeira (if using; if not, increase water to 1/2 cup) and use a wooden spoon to scrape the bottom of the pan. Reduce the heat to low and cook for 25 to 30 minutes, stirring occasionally. Add more water, 1/4 cup at a time if the pan is too dry. Season with pepper to taste. Transfer to a bowl to cool. The onions will keep for up to 4 days in the refrigerator or in the freezer for up to 3 months.

Notes: I like to use big, softball-size Spanish onions for this, which not only minimizes the prep (because there are fewer onions to peel and slice) but also results in a bit more texture in the final recipe. You can substitute smaller yellow onions, but you'll need roughly twice as many, depending on their size. Just aim for the same weight.

BÉCHAMEL SAUCE
Makes about 4 cups

Béchamel, or *besciamella*, as it's known in Italian, sounds fancy but is a snap to make. This versatile sauce comes in handy for the lasagna on page 175 or for any kind of a vegetable gratin. To transport yourself to a Parisian bistro, roast halved heads of Belgian endive until soft, add some béchamel and the cheese of your choice, and broil until brown and bubbly.

INGREDIENTS

4 tablespoons (1/2 stick) unsalted butter
1/3 cup all-purpose flour
3 1/2 cups whole milk, hot
1 teaspoon kosher salt
Big pinch of cayenne pepper

VEG FORWARD

Freshly ground pepper (optional)
Freshly ground nutmeg

INSTRUCTIONS

Melt the butter in a medium saucepan over medium heat. Add the flour and cook, stirring until the mixture sizzles and turns a slightly darker shade, about 3 to 4 minutes.

Slowly pour in the hot milk, whisking all the while, until smooth. Continue whisking to avoid scorching the bottom, until you start to see bubbles on the surface. Reduce the heat and cook, stirring, for 3 to 4 minutes, until slightly thickened. Season with the salt, cayenne, pepper (if using), and nutmeg and whisk thoroughly to combine.

If not using right away, pour into a bowl or container and whisk frequently to cool it somewhat. Then cover until ready to use. There's no need to press the plastic onto the surface to keep a skin from forming; the steam that forms under the plastic will do the trick.

Note: If you need to veganize the sauce, you can use olive oil instead of butter and any kind of alternative milk instead of cow's milk.

SALTED CANDIED HAZELNUTS
Makes 1 cup

These salty-sweet, candied nuts elevate any fruit dessert by adding an irresistible crunch. They were purpose-built for the Rhubarb and Hazelnut Frangipane Galettes on page 43, but they'd be fantastic just sprinkled over a bowl of ice cream.

INGREDIENTS

1/2 cup/67 g whole raw hazelnuts
2 teaspoons unsalted butter, plus more for greasing the parchment
1/4 cup/52 g granulated sugar
1/2 teaspoon vanilla extract
1/4 teaspoon flaky salt

INSTRUCTIONS

Heat the oven to 350°F. Toast the hazelnuts for 8 to 10 minutes, until they smell toasty, the skins are popping off, and they are turning golden. Remove from the oven and pour into a bowl. Cover the bowl with a folded dishcloth and let the nuts cool. Rub off as much of the skin as comes off easily. Separate the nuts from the skins and discard the skins. Very coarsely chop the nuts.

Butter a piece of parchment or a silicone baking mat and lay it on the counter. In a medium skillet, combine the hazelnuts, sugar, butter, and vanilla. Cook over medium-high heat, stirring occasionally, until the nuts are toasted and the sugar is liquified and dark amber, 5 to 7 minutes. Pour out on the parchment and spread into a single layer. Immediately sprinkle with flaky salt and let cool. When cooled, chop into smaller pieces.

GREEN TAHINI-YOGURT "EVERYTHING SAUCE"
Makes 1 1/2 cups

So named because it goes with everything. It's great on roasted veggies, especially Shaved Cauliflower (page 147), and it's also delicious on a piece of meaty white fish like halibut, or on salmon or chicken. We love it on grain bowl dinners. It also keeps exceptionally well, so you'll find plenty of things to use it on.

INGREDIENTS

1 cup thick yogurt (like Greek or Skyr)
1 cup (packed) fresh herbs, such as dill, cilantro, parsley, or basil
2 scallions, roughly chopped
3 tablespoons tahini
2 tablespoons lemon juice (from 1 lemon)
1/2 teaspoon kosher salt, plus more to taste
2 teaspoons Yondu (see page xvi, optional) or fish sauce
About 2 tablespoons warm water

INSTRUCTIONS

Combine the yogurt, herbs, scallions, tahini, lemon juice, salt, and Yondu or fish sauce (if using) in a food processor and pulse until completely smooth.

Add water as needed to thin to desired consistency. It will keep in an airtight container for at least a week.

PEA PESTO
Makes about 1 cup

Pea pesto has magical powers, especially on pasta, where the starch in the peas helps make a creamy sauce when mixed with a little reserved pasta water as in Bucatini with Pea Pesto, Ricotta, and Shaved Asparagus on page 7. It can also be used as a toast topping or swirled into soup.

INGREDIENTS
1 cup fresh or thawed frozen peas
1 garlic clove or 1 stalk green garlic
1/2 cup finely grated pecorino or Parmesan cheese or a combination, plus more for serving
1 cup loosely packed herbs, such as mint, basil, and/or parsley
1/4 cup extra-virgin olive oil, or more as needed
1/2 teaspoon kosher salt
Freshly ground pepper

INSTRUCTIONS
Combine the peas, garlic, cheese, herbs, oil, salt, and pepper in a food processor. Pulse until a coarse puree is formed. Add more oil as needed to loosen.

The pesto will keep in the refrigerator for 3 days or in the freezer for up to 3 months.

TOMATILLO SALSA (SALSA VERDE)
Makes 5 cups

Enjoy salsa verde on its own as a dip with chips, on breakfast tacos or any other kind of tacos, and on nachos, chilaquiles, egg dishes, and in Green Veggie Enchiladas (page 127).

INGREDIENTS
2 pounds tomatillos (about 24)
3 large garlic cloves, peeled
1 white onion, roughly chopped
1/2 large jalapeño, seeds removed, cut into large pieces
1 teaspoon vegetable oil
1 cup lightly packed cilantro leaves
1 1/2 teaspoons kosher salt

INSTRUCTIONS
Heat the broiler, with a rack about 8 inches away. Line a baking sheet with foil.

Toss the tomatillos, garlic, onion, and jalapeño with the oil to lightly coat them.

Broil until everything is lightly charred, tossing once or twice, about 10 minutes.

Let cool slightly and transfer to a blender. Add the cilantro and salt and blend until smooth. The salsa can be refrigerated for up to 4 days or frozen for up to 6 months.

Notes: It's tricky to say how much of a fresh chili to use in a recipe since heat levels can vary so much. There's nothing worse than whizzing something up in the blender to find that it is way too hot. For that reason, I suggest that you *very* gingerly taste a fresh chili, just touching your tongue to a small slice and waiting a moment to assess the heat level. If it's very spicy, add less than the recipe calls for and proceed with caution.

VEG FORWARD

CHARRED TOMATO VINAIGRETTE
Makes about ½ cup

This unique vinaigrette gets a hint of smoke from the charring, which can be done on the grill or under the broiler, as well as plenty of natural sweetness and acidity from the tomatoes. It's great on greens of any kind, and it makes a saucy but not oily dressing for Grilled Three-Bean Salad (page 95) or Warm Weather Farro Bowls with Grilled Tofu (page 5).

INGREDIENTS
1 pint cherry or grape tomatoes
1 garlic clove
2 tablespoons red wine vinegar
2 tablespoons extra-virgin olive oil
Kosher salt and freshly ground pepper

INSTRUCTIONS
Preheat a gas grill to medium. Heat a grill basket or grill wok and add the tomatoes. Cook them, tossing occasionally, until charred and softened, about 10 minutes.

Transfer the tomatoes to a small bowl and, using a Microplane, grate the garlic into the tomatoes and mix it in. (The residual heat from the tomatoes will soften the raw taste of the garlic.) Add the vinegar, oil, and salt and pepper to taste and mix well. Let marinate for 10 to 15 minutes.

Push the tomato mixture through a fine-mesh sieve and discard the solids. Adjust the seasonings to taste.

To cook the tomatoes in the oven, line a small baking sheet with foil, position a rack 6 inches from the broiler, and broil the tomatoes until charred and softened, 6 to 8 minutes.

PICKLED SHALLOT VINAIGRETTE
Makes 1 ¼ cups

This is an almost classic vinaigrette, the key difference being that the shallots are lightly pickled by being briefly heated in the vinegar base. Cooking them ever so slightly helps them soak up the flavor of the vinegar and takes the raw edge off. This recipe makes a big batch, one that will happily live in your fridge (preferably in a glass jar) for a week or so, ready to dress just about anything, including a last-minute green salad to go with dinner or the French Vegetable Salad on page 25. If you want to add fresh herbs, add them just before using.

INGREDIENTS
1 medium shallot, minced (about ½ cup)
¼ cup red wine vinegar
¼ teaspoon kosher salt
Freshly ground pepper
2 tablespoons lemon juice
1 tablespoon honey Dijon mustard
1 tablespoon Dijon mustard
¼ cup neutral oil, like grapeseed or safflower
6 tablespoons extra-virgin olive oil

INSTRUCTIONS
Combine the shallot, vinegar, salt, and pepper in a glass jar, a microwave-safe bowl, or a small saucepan if you don't have a microwave. Heat for 40 seconds in the microwave and let stand until slightly cooler. Alternatively, heat the mixture on the stovetop.

Add the lemon juice and the mustards, close the jar, and shake vigorously, or if using a bowl, use a fork or small whisk to blend.

Add the oils and again, shake vigorously until the dressing is emulsified, or whisk the oil in gradually if using a bowl. Store in the refrigerator for a week or more.

Notes: Whisk in a tablespoon or two of any of these for a creamier dressing and a different flavor: tahini, Greek yogurt, sour cream, peanut butter or sun butter, or miso.

MISO-MAPLE DRESSING
Makes ¾ cup

This tasty, slightly sweet dressing is especially good on a kale salad or drizzled over your grain bowl.

INGREDIENTS
¼ cup lemon juice
1 small garlic clove, grated on a Microplane, or
1 teaspoon roasted garlic
1 tablespoon tahini
2 teaspoons maple syrup
1 tablespoon white miso
¼ teaspoon kosher salt
Freshly ground pepper
¼ cup extra-virgin olive oil

INSTRUCTIONS
Combine the lemon juice, garlic, tahini, maple syrup, miso, salt, and pepper in a small bowl. Use a fork to combine thoroughly.

Slowly drizzle in the oil, using the fork to incorporate it.

VEGETABLE STOCK
Makes about 6 cups

Homemade vegetable stock is so much more full-flavored than anything you can buy, not to mention much cheaper. Just save your vegetable scraps (mushroom stems, carrot stubs, fennel stalks) as you're cooking and throw them in a bag in your freezer until you're ready to make stock.

INGREDIENTS
1 tablespoon olive oil
2 carrots, cut into 1-inch pieces
1 stalk celery, cut into 1-inch pieces
1 large yellow onion, skin on and cut into 8 wedges
1 leek or spring onion (or 6 scallions), cut into small pieces

Fennel stalks from 1 bulb, roughly chopped
4 large mushrooms, quartered, or mushroom stems
A few cherry tomatoes or ½ tomato, cut into a few pieces
4 garlic cloves
Handful of parsley stems and or leaves
A few sprigs of fresh thyme
1 bay leaf
½ teaspoon black peppercorns
¼ ounce dried porcini (scant ½ cup)
12 cups water
Parmesan rind (optional)
¾ teaspoon kosher salt, plus more to taste

INSTRUCTIONS
Heat the olive oil in a medium Dutch oven or stock pot over medium-high heat. Add the carrots, celery, onion, leek, fennel, mushrooms, tomatoes, garlic, parsley, thyme, bay leaf, peppercorns, and porcini. Sauté for 8 to 10 minutes to wilt slightly. Add the Parmesan rind (if using) and the salt. Add the water and bring to a boil, lower the heat, and simmer for 1 hour and 15 minutes, stirring occasionally, until flavorful. Turn off the heat and cool for about 30 minutes.

Strain through a fine-mesh sieve into a bowl and let cool. Use right away or refrigerate in airtight containers or jars. Once it's chilled, you can freeze the containers for future use.

CORN COB STOCK
Makes 6 cups

Yellow onion skins help to give it a golden color, so throw those in. If you have a Parmesan rind around, put it in too, as it will add some richness and depth of flavor.

INGREDIENTS
4 corn cobs
20 black peppercorns
1 sprig thyme
1 sprig parsley
1 large garlic clove, smashed
1 small onion, quartered
1 bay leaf
10 cups water

VEG FORWARD

INSTRUCTIONS

Combine all the ingredients in a large saucepan and bring to a boil. Reduce the heat so it simmers and cook for 1 to 1 1/2 hours. Let cool slightly before straining.

Discard the solids and refrigerate the stock if not using right away. Refrigerate for up to 4 days or freeze for up to 6 months.

TOMATO WATER
Makes about 3 cups

Tomato water looks like nothing much, but its flavor is the pure distilled essence of tomato. This is a lovely thing to make when you're overwhelmed with tomatoes. Freeze your scraps or about-to-be-overripe tomatoes, so you can make it on your own schedule. Use it to make Tomato Water Lemonade (page 75) or Watermelon, Cucumber, and Tomato Water Salad (page 85).

INGREDIENTS

3 1/2 pounds ripe, peak-season tomatoes of any kind, cut into chunks

INSTRUCTIONS

Freeze the tomatoes on a parchment- or wax-paper-lined baking sheet. When they're completely frozen, transfer to a gallon zip-top bag if not making the tomato water right away. You can freeze the tomatoes for up to a few months.

When ready to use, rinse a large piece of cheesecloth with water and line a large sieve or colander with it. Fill the sieve with the frozen tomatoes and set it over a large, deep bowl. Let sit at room temperature until the tomatoes are completely defrosted, 2 to 3 hours.

Place the bowl and the sieve in the refrigerator overnight. As the tomatoes soften, gently twist the cheesecloth over top of the tomatoes to compress them lightly, but don't squeeze too hard. You want to help extract as much of the clear liquid as possible, but if you squeeze it will become cloudy. As the bowl fills with liquid, pour it off into a separate container so the bottom of the sieve isn't sitting in the liquid.

ACKNOWLEDGMENTS

There are many people to thank for their help and support in bringing this book to fruition.

None of it would be possible without my agent, David Black, and everyone else at DBA who helped in some way. Thanks for always believing in me and having my back.

To my publisher, Harper Celebrate, thank you for catching this curve ball and caring so much about it. I'm so lucky this book found a loving home with you. Michael Aulisio, Marilyn Jansen, Bonnie Honeycutt, Tiffany Forrester, Kristen Sasamoto, MacKenzie Collier, Robin Richardson, and Lydia Eagle (and everyone else behind the scenes), thanks for helping to make this book in record time and get it out into the world.

To my editor, Rux Martin, thank you so much for taking this book on at the last minute and being such a thorough and tireless editor. I am lucky to have gotten the chance to work with a veteran like you! The book is so much better with your fingerprint on it. You saved the day!

To Andrea Fleck-Nisbet, thank you for your interest in this book and your belief in me. I'm sorry we didn't get to see this one through together.

To Cybele Grandjean, thank you for your sophisticated, gorgeous, yet friendly design. I love it.

To Tara Sgoi, thanks for taking pictures of me in my element, both in the fields and in the kitchen.

To Frankie (Francesca) Crichton, you know I couldn't have done this without you! Thanks for keeping everything organized, tweaking the photographs, and giving me feedback, especially about what made you the hungriest.

To Alaina Chou, if it wasn't for this book, we wouldn't have met, and I'm so glad we did! Thank you for helping me with takeoff and landing and everything in between. You are a gem.

Eva Karagiorgas and Mona Creative, thank you for helping to spread the word about vegging forward. I'm so happy we finally got to work together, three years after our first attempt.

ACKNOWLEDGMENTS

To Maryann Pomeranz, thank you for being such a diligent and thorough recipe tester. I can sleep better at night knowing the recipes have been put through their paces by you.

Andrea Gentl, you gave me the confidence to shoot this book myself, and for that I thank you. I asked you if I was crazy to do it, and you assured me that it would be "totally awesome" and "an amazing project"—and it was!

To all the people who amaze me and inspire me and teach me, thank you. To name just a few: Claudia Fleming, Frances Boswell, Aran Goyoaga, Lia Ronnen, Maria Robledo, Maya Kaimal, Rebecca Jurkevich, and Ayesha Patel.

To my husband, Steve, thank you for all your love and support. I love being a team with you. Thank you for all your harvesting at Quail Hill and for your enthusiasm for vegetables and food in general. Your always honest (and usually positive) reviews of my recipes are invaluable.

The biggest thank you for this book goes to all the hard-working farmers whose produce never ceases to inspire and delight us. You do so much to provide nourishment and comfort with resourcefulness, creativity, grit, and grace. To name just a few: Marilee's Farmstand, Pike's, The Green Thumb, Amber Waves, Halsey Farm, Norwich Meadows Farm, Mountain Sweet Berry Farm, Campo Rosso Farm, and Quail Hill Farm, our CSA, where we walk the fields and get a taste of what hard but satisfying work it is to produce food.

VEG FORWARD

INDEX

VEG FORWARD

ABOUT THE AUTHOR

SUSAN SPUNGEN is a cook, food stylist, recipe developer, and author. She was the founding food editor and editorial director for food at Martha Stewart Living Omnimedia from its inception until 2003. She was the culinary consultant and food stylist on the feature films *Julie & Julia*, *It's Complicated*, and *Eat, Pray, Love*. She is the author of *Open Kitchen: Inspired Food for Casual Gatherings*, *Recipes: A Collection for the Modern Cook*, *What's a Hostess to Do?*, and *Strawberries (a Short Stack Edition)*. She is the author of *Susanality* (a popular Substack newsletter) and is a frequent contributor to NYT Cooking. She lives in New York City and East Hampton, New York.